The Freshwater Angler™

COMPLETE PHOTO GUIDE TO
FLY TYING
300 Tips, Techniques and Methods

C. Boyd Pfeiffer

**Creative Publishing
international**

Chanhassen, Minnesota

C. Boyd Pfeiffer, an award-winning outdoor journalist and photographer, has been published in more than 70 magazines, including *Saltwater Fly Fishing, Outdoor Life, American Angler*. He has authored 23 books on fishing and outdoor photography. He lives in Phoenix, Maryland.

To Brenda

**Creative Publishing
international**

President/CEO: Ken Fund
Vice President/Publisher: Linda Ball
Vice President/Retail Sales & Marketing: Kevin Haas
Executive Editor, Outdoor Group: Barbara Harold
Creative Director: Brad Springer
Book Designer: Kari Johnston
Project Manager: Tracy Stanley
Production Manager: Laura Hokkanen
Production Staff: Helga Thielen

Printed in China
10 9 8 7 6 5 4 3 2 1

COMPLETE PHOTO GUIDE TO FLY TYING
by C. Boyd Pfeiffer

All photographs copyright © 2006 C. Boyd Pfeiffer; except Front Cover (large) and pages 5, 6, 32, 42, 62, 74, 102 © 2006 Creative Publishing international.

Angler quotations reproduced with permission from *The Quotable Fisherman* by Nick Lyons, The Lyons Press, ©1998.

NOTE: Fly tying involves small flies and tying materials. For this reason and for photo clarity, many procedures and steps have been photographed using larger-than-normal hooks and materials, and sometimes brighter or more visible threads to help show and explain the procedures illustrated.

Library of Congress Cataloging-in-Publication Data

Pfeiffer, C. Boyd.
  Complete photo guide to fly tying : tips, techniques, and methods / C. Boyd Pfeiffer.
      p. cm.
  Includes index.
  ISBN 1-58923-221-6 (hard cover)
  1. Fly tying. 2. Fly tying—Pictorial works. I. Title.
  SH451.P482 2005
  688.7'9124'022—dc22   2005008191

TABLE OF CONTENTS

Introduction

*T*hink of a tip as a shortcut or improved way of doing something. Tips in any field are concise bits of information that relay a better, faster, simpler way of doing something. In the case of this book, that something is tying flies.

Tying flies is a consuming hobby, one that can have fly fishermen involving their non-fishing hours into the search for the best possible fly, the simplest way to tie, the best way to make a sure-fire offering for a sure-fire way to catch a fish—whether it be a trout, panfish, bass, inshore striper, offshore billfish, or anything between these extremes. Anglers practice fly tying for all of these species, along with flies for pike, musky, snook, tarpon, bonefish, walleye, shad, and even catfish and carp.

In some cases, a fly-tying tip can be as simple as substituting clear nail polish for head cement. In others, it might be a little more complicated, such as adding tungsten powder to the epoxy head sealer to weight a fly a new way or methods of extending a hook shank length to making long pencil poppers. It can be snelling a hook to tie a tandem fly or using ink blotters as a background when fly tying to ease your eyes.

You can find tips in all the myriad aspects of tying, from tying the thread onto the hook to sealing the head with head cement or placing a fly with an epoxied head on a fly rotator.

To make for a hopefully easy reference, I've divided this book into chapters covering basic areas of fly tying. Thus, you can turn to that section if you have a particularly vexing problem in a given area of tying, or just peruse the book for tips and tricks that you can pick up for future tying.

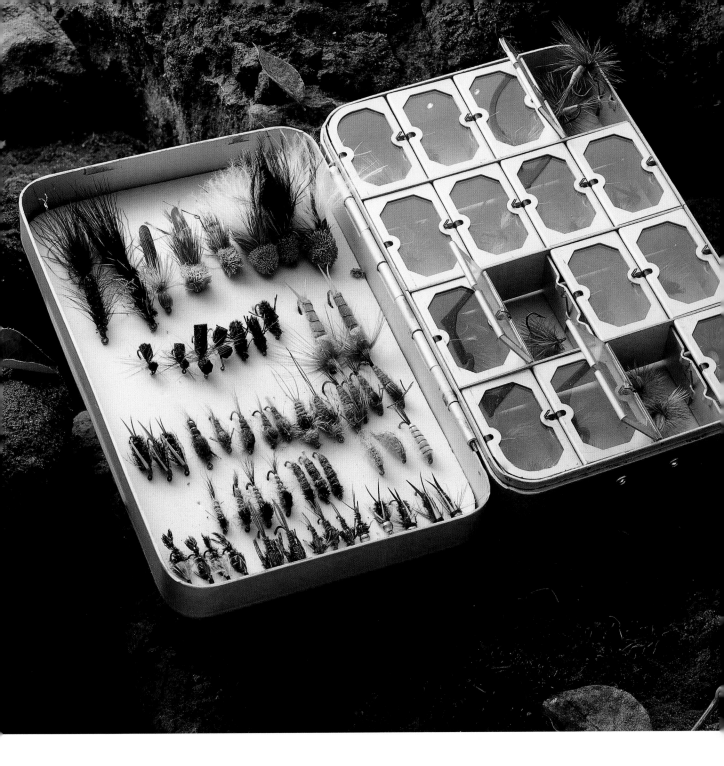

The main purpose of this book is not to be a complete treatise on fly tying—many excellent books on this are available—but to include those tricks and techniques that are often outside the normal range of fly tying, and outside the standard or accepted ways of accomplishing some fly-tying task. Enjoy these ideas, so many of which others have taught me and shared with me, and pass them on to your fly-tying friends.

C. Boyd Pfeiffer

Chapter 1

Getting Started

1 FLY-TYING BACKGROUND

Clean, plain backgrounds are necessary when tying flies. A cluttered background distracts from the view of the small fly you are tying.

For best results, use a background plate or easel. You can buy them or make your own from a clear plastic commercial sign holder (available in several sizes from office supply stores). Use a spring clip to hold plain-colored poster board or matte-finish board on the easel as a background for your fly.

2 BACKGROUND BOARDS

For best results, use light colors for your background boards for fly tying. For a change of pace and to relieve eyestrain, use different colors and switch off periodically.

Good colors are pastels, such as white, light blue, light green, tan, light gray, etc. If you are tying very light colored or white flies, you might wish to switch to a dark blue or black matte board for contrast with the fly.

3 STACKER PROTECTION

One way to keep a stacker (hair evener) from harming your fly-tying bench is to glue a patch of rubber gasket material to the base. Cut out the rubber gasket material to the shape of the stacker base and glue it to the bottom. Gasket material is available anywhere auto supplies are sold.

Alternatives to the gasket material are the thin foams available in craft and art stores, and inner tube patches. Use any flexible glue such as Pliobond, Ultra Flex, or contact cement. You can also use a square of gasket material on your tying bench as a pounding surface on which to hit the stacker to even hair and fur.

4 STORAGE

If you have trouble storing beads, check out the bins and containers at craft and art stores for this purpose. You can get racks of bins in several sizes, both as to the individual bin size and also the number of compartments that are in each rack. Most sell for only a few dollars and also allow stacking of the racks for those using a lot of beads in their tying.

5 BUYING YARN

If you tie lots of flies of one type and color, good body materials are available at any sewing, knitting, or craft shop. For the quantity that you get, the materials are far cheaper than similar materials from any fly shop. These shops carry yarn and other stranded materials in many sizes, materials, colors, and textures.

The one problem with these is that they are usually available only in large spools or skeins that would be more material than any flytier would ever use. One solution is to purchase materials with your fly-tying buddies, or a fly fishing/fly tying club, then divide the materials into manageable lengths and split the cost with those involved. You can all get a lot of material for a little cash this way.

6 HANDLING WASTE

Lefty Kreh recently came up with a neat idea for handling fly-tying waste. Instead of using one of the bags that are difficult to empty, he mounted a waste container to the pull-out drawer of his fly-tying desk.

To make the waste container, he used a short length of 4-inch-diameter (10.2-cm) PVC pipe (like solid drainpipe), cut it and a pipe cap in half lengthwise, and then cut it to fit the width of his drawer. He glued the cap into place on one end and added a half-circle wood "plug" to the other; the plug held in the PVC half pipe with a dowel through holes drilled in the PVC and the wood plug.

You can sweep the waste off of the table and into the PVC trough, which you can empty into a garbage can by removing the wood plug and sweeping out the contents.

7 FLY-TYING COMFORT

Physical therapists may tell you that fly tying is not a good "job" to have, and that it is detrimental to rotator cuff muscles and posture, and can cause back problems. (The same goes for fly casting, but that is a different story.) To prevent injury, have a definite fly-tying work area with a comfortable chair, large work surface, and a vise at a comfortable position. Professionals tell you to place the vise jaws slightly above elbow height and about forearm length or less in front of you. Take lots of breaks when tying flies, and stretch and rotate your arms when possible.

8 PROTECTING NATURAL MATERIALS

To store natural materials and protect them from insects, place them in an airtight container, such as Tupperware. Make sure that there are no insects in the materials and add some moth flakes or mothballs when sealing them for storage.

9 USING MOTHBALLS

Mothballs or moth flakes can adhere to fly-tying materials, making them unusable. To prevent this, keep the moth repellent separate from the fly-tying materials, even when in the same airtight storage box. One way to do this is to keep the moth repellent in an open plastic bag next to the fly-tying materials stored a box. This way they can't come in contact with each other, but you've protected the fly-tying materials with the fumes. You can also place the mothballs in a small open card-board box or mailing envelope. If you use an envelope, punch some holes through the envelope to allow the mothball fumes to escape and protect the materials. You could also use a 35mm film canister punched with holes. With mothballs in the closed canister, fumes escape through the holes to protect materials without direct contact.

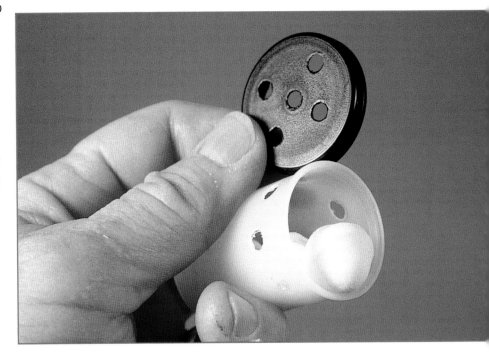

10 BUYING FABRIC

If you plan to buy fabric, make sure that you do not overbuy. Most fabric that you use (vinyl, cloth-backed vinyl, suede, Ultra Suede, fleece, felt, etc.) is sold in bolts that are 36 to 54 inches (91.4 to 137.2 cm) wide. However, you do not need to buy an entire yard of cloth. Most stores will sell you an eighth of a yard (12 cm), reducing the cost of most materials to only a few bucks at most. You still receive 4 1/2 inches (11.4 cm) times the width of the material bolt—a lot of material for tying flies.

11 STORING BULK MATERIALS

If you have a lot of bulk fly-tying materials, an ideal way to store them is in plastic containers such as shoeboxes and sweater boxes. These are readily available from general and discount stores. They are not airtight, so be sure to add mothballs to any boxes containing natural materials. To know what you have in each box, use self-stick labels from an office supply store to label each box with a black felt-tip pen.

12 PREVENTING EYESTRAIN

To prevent eyestrain from glare while tying flies, place a matte-finish desk blotter on your worktable. Desk blotters are available in soft colors, are non-glare, and are inexpensive. You can easily replace them if you spill head cement. You can get these in colors from art and office supply stores, with green always a good choice (but keep several colors on hand). A good guide is to use a color that contrasts with your materials.

"...fly tying is the next best thing to fishing; it is the sort of licking of the lips that eases a thirsty man in the desert."

Arthur Ransome
"Fly Tying in Winter" Rod and Line (1929)

13 SAVING SAMPLES

If you like a particular fly-tying material, cut off a short length or piece of it and staple or tape it to a 3- by 5-inch (7.6- by 12.7-cm) index card. Label the card with the important information such as material, brand, color, manufacturer, supplier, price, etc., so that you can order more when you run out. Make sample cards for all materials that are unusual or rare and store the cards with materials in a plastic index card box or file.

14 STRONG LIGHT

Use a good, bright light when tying flies. Incandescent lights are fine, either in a standard desk light or one of the small halogen lights. Small halogen lights provide a lot of light in a given area, but can get hot. Keep this in mind for summer-time use.

15 STICKING WITH SIMPLE PATTERNS

If you design your own flies and are interested in flies that catch fish, stick with simple impressionistic patterns rather than attempting exact copies of the natural insect. Most expert fly-tiers, even if tying the exact imitations for "show," display, competition, or framing, use simple, fuzzy, buggy-looking flies for their fishing.

16 MULTIPLE LIGHTS

Use several lights for best results when tying flies. Multiple lights provide light from different angles, so that you are less likely to have a distracting shadow that impairs your ability to see the fly or study a specific operation.

17 STORING MATERIALS STRAIGHT

Materials stored bent or twisted stay bent and twisted. This applies to both natural materials like necks, skins, and such, along with synthetics such as Super Hair and Unique. This makes fly tying difficult, if not impossible with these materials, since you can't get them to lie and look right on the fly. Thus, store all materials in containers that are large enough to allow the material to lie flat.

18 SUNLIGHT-BALANCED LIGHT

Lights such as the Giraffe Light and Ott-Lite provide sunlight-balanced illumination of your flies so that you can see your fly materials exactly as they appear in the sun and to fish.

19 ORGANIZING STRANDED MATERIALS

Craft stores sell small plastic boxes with cards included for wrapping and storing stranded materials such as yarn, chenille, floss, etc. These are ideal for storing a large number of different colors of these materials. The cards fit into the compartments in the plastic box. You can re-spool any materials from their original packaging onto these cards to make a system with one box containing all the colors of a given material. Label the box to indicate the contents.

20 PREPARING MATERIALS IN ADVANCE

Tying up a bunch of the same fly in the same size? Streamline your operation by first preparing all the materials that you need—selecting the hackles, tail fibers, wings, etc., of the same size, and laying out the other materials—body, ribbing, tinsel, throat, etc.—that you use for that pattern. By having available all the materials for a quantity of flies, you streamline operations and save time selecting hackle, tails, body material, etc., each time for each fly. Commercial flytiers often use this trick when tying large quantities of one fly of one size. You can also use it for as few as a half-dozen flies.

"…neither time nor repetition has destroyed the illusion that the rise of a trout to a dry fly is properly regarded in the light of a miracle."

Harold Blaisdell
The Philosophical Fisherman (1969)

21 COUNTING TAILS OR LEGS

Got a few more tails in your flies than on the natural insect? Got a few more legs than the six that insects are equipped with? Don't worry—fish can't count. What you want is a fair approximation of what their meals look like. When tying a dry fly, you want it to float well in the surface film. This often requires more tails than the natural insect has, and a far thicker hackle than is warranted by the six legs of an insect.

22 SAMPLE FLIES

When you tie a new pattern of fly that you like, tie several and keep one as a sample for future reference. Keep these samples in a small plastic bag, and store with an index card listing the pattern recipe. To protect the fly, you may wish to keep dry flies, some nymphs, and similar structured flies in a container, such as an empty 35-mm film canister or empty hook box.

23 SMALLER FLIES MEAN SMALLER MATERIALS

When tying flies smaller than you normally tie, you will need to shorten, slim, and scale down the materials. This requires smaller hackle, shorter tails, thinner dubbing or body material, and even thinner tinsel ribbing. It also means fewer bucktail or synthetic fibers in a wing, and fewer strands of flash on the side of a fly.

24 EXAMINING FLIES FROM ALL SIDES

Examine each fly that you tie from both sides as you tie it to make sure that it is symmetrical. This is especially important if adding flash to wings, positioning a wing or throat, or similar steps. Mistakes are much easier to correct when the fly is still in the vise and the thread is still on the hook than after finishing and sealing the fly head. One easy way to do this is with a rotating vise that allows you to easily check both sides of the fly.

25 STORING NECKS

You can store fly-tying necks in a file cabinet. Place each neck in a clean plastic bag and then in a manila folder. If you like, you can even label the folder so that you have a filing and identification system. Then place several folders in a hanging Pendaflex folder to keep them flat and straight. Do not use a "box bottom" hanging folder, since this allows the necks to sag and bend, damaging them for fly tying.

28 COMBING OUT UNDERFUR

Use a moustache comb, available from any drug store, to comb out the underfur of deer hair and other natural furs from which you want the underfur removed. The moustache comb is ideal, not only for removing the underfur before tying with the guard hairs (bucktail streamers, deer body fur bass bugs, etc.), but also to collect underfur to use for dubbing. You can use underfur like this by itself for dubbing or mix it with other furs or synthetic materials to make a mixed dubbing.

26 CAPTURING FLOATING INSECTS

One easy way to capture floating or emerging insects is to use window screen, fine mesh screen, or tulle from a fabric store to catch nymphs and emerging duns from the surface film. Secure the netting material to a frame. A good, simple frame to use is a friction-fit frame designed to hold needlepoint or tatting material and available from craft or sewing stores. To use along the water surface, hold the frame half under at an angle to capture insects. To capture underwater aquatic insects, hold the frame underwater touching the bottom and dislodge some rocks upstream to free insects to drift into the net.

27 WASHING NATURAL MATERIALS

If you use materials that you get from hunters or road kills (be careful and check local regulations for this), you should wash the materials and dry them before storage.

To do this, wash necks, furs, and skins in a mild detergent, rinse thoroughly, and then dry. Dry by hanging outside from a clothesline and make sure that they are hanging in the shade to prevent the sun from causing residual fat to liquefy. Once the materials are completely dry, store them flat with mothballs in a suitable container.

29 COLLECTING INSECTS

Some anglers and flytiers get heavily involved in aquatic entomology; others do not. In any case, it helps to have on hand a few insects to use as examples when tying flies.

To do this, use a fine-mesh net to dip insects from the water, capture them while they are floating, or net them in the air as they are flying. To get nymph forms of insects, wade the shallows and lift over a few rocks to gather mayflies, caddis cases, and stonefly nymphs from the rocks. Turn the rock back to its normal position when finished so that you don't harm the remaining insects.

You can also use your net to capture emerging insects along with mature insects flying and mating. Place all insects in small bottles with rubbing alcohol for future reference. Label as to time, date, and place captured. Later you can add further information as to type, or genus, and species.

Alcohol (and formaldehyde used by professionals) will fade the colors on the insects, so make separate notes as to color or check with books for suggestions when tying your own patterns.

30 TYING SMALL FLIES

If you have trouble tying small flies, start by tying some of the same pattern, but in larger sizes. After you are comfortable with tying the flies, move to tying them in the next size down until you reach the size you desire. This allows you to develop and perfect your skills gradually. Realize that each time you go to a smaller size, you also reduce the size of the materials incorporated into the fly.

31 GARBAGE BAG SCUD BACKS

Plastic garbage bags make excellent scud backs for small flies. Get the thickest material that you can and cut into thin strips—about 1/8 to 1/4 inch (3 to 6 mm) wide—for scud backs. Plastic bag material is available in basic colors such as black, brown, white, yellow, and clear to give you a choice when tying different types of scuds and freshwater shrimp.

32 PREVENTING EYESTRAIN

To prevent eyestrain, dull the highly polished metal finishes on the vise using fine steel wool or even gun bluing to reduce glare. This usually only works on ferrous metals—it does not work on stainless steel or certain brass fittings. A quick and removable substitute for this is to cover the post of the vise with a dull tape, such as masking tape.

33 A TIP FROM LEFTY KREH

Joe Brooks, well-known outdoor writer and mentor, introduced me to fly fishing in 1947. I became immediately addicted to it. In the nearly 60 years since that time I have been lucky enough to fish over much of the planet in both fresh and saltwater.

There are many things that keep fly fishing as fresh in my heart and mind as in 1947. I think the most important is that I continually keep learning. An example I often cite to young outdoor writers concerns a young man at a California fishing clinic. During the 1950s I became interested in knots and over several years a huge amount of data was amassed. Using this information with Mark Sosin we co-authored a book published in the early 1970s that is still in print.

Our publisher, Nick Lyons, insisted that we only include 40 knots, but they had to cover everything from using cable for offshore billfishing to tying with an 8X tippet. Over the next ten years or so after the book came out scores of people showed me knots that weren't in the book. I was force fed the information and knew as many knots as almost anyone.

During a clinic in California I demonstrated nine ways to attach a leader to a fly line. Each took several minutes to tie. I asked if there were any questions and a young man raised his hand. "Yes, son, what is it?" He answered, "I think I have a better way." I said, "Well, get up here and show us."

The lad took a needle, a piece of fly line and a leader butt section and in about 12 seconds handed me a perfect nail knot. I turned to audience and said, "Forget what this expert showed you and let's find out what this young man did."

It was there that I learned to tie the speedy nail knot, which I have shared with many others. The important point to be made is a near-world expert on a subject can learn something from even a 12-year-old boy.

That is just one reason I love the sport of fly fishing.

Chapter 2

Tools & How To Use Them

34 VISE ANGLE

If you are tying small flies and need more room for handling materials, try adjusting the angle of the vise (if possible) to a steeper angle. This allows more room for your fingers to handle materials and hold materials in position on the hook for tying.

35 CHECKING FLIES

If you do not have a rotating vise, but still want to check both sides of a fly as you tie it, keep a small-handled cosmetic mirror on your fly-tying bench. This allows you to hold the mirror up to see the far side of the fly without the time-consuming task of taking it out of the vise.

36 CHECKING SMALL FLIES

When tying very small flies or if you have trouble with your eyes, consider using a magnifier. Fly shops sell magnifiers made exclusively for fly tying, but you can also get the same thing from office supply stores. Some magnifiers also have a built-in circular fluorescent rim light to provide lighting for the fly. The magnifiers that fit on your head are particularly useful. They move with you and do not add another piece of equipment between you and the vise.

37 MAKING THROATS

To make a throat on a streamer fly or wet fly, use a rotary vise. Turn the vise jaws 180 degrees to position the fly hook point up. (If your vise does not rotate, remove the hook and replace it upside down.) This makes it easier to tie in a throat, since you will be using the soft loop method and pulling the thread down on the throat rather than up as if tying it without the hook reversed. This is far easier and makes for a more secure tie, while also allowing you to make sure that you line up the throat with the hook shank.

38 INEXPENSIVE HALF-HITCH TOOL

The front end of an inexpensive empty ballpoint pen makes a fine half-hitch tool. The best types are those with the clicker cap to extend/retract the ink point.

Unscrew the pen and discard all but the tapered plastic or metal end. The tip end fits over the eye of small flies and the taper allows you to easily slide off half hitches after you wrap the thread around the barrel of the pen. If you have several of these, drill out one or two to larger size holes to fit larger hooks.

39 TYING SMALL FLIES

To see flies easily, get reading glasses designed for the distance you work from your fly-tying vise. You might be able to use the inexpensive models available from most stores if you do not have any serious eye problems and if both eyes need about the same correction. Measure the distance from your eyes to the fly-tying vise at home, and then choose glasses that work well at that distance.

40 NATURAL FLOAT FLIES

To make a fly float lower in the surface film, use scissors to trim the bottom hackle. The result is a fly in which the tail, body, and hackle are all floating in the surface film, thus more closely imitating an emerging mayfly. This is basically what Comparadun flies do.

41 CLAMP AND BOARD

If you don't have a pedestal vise, but travel and take your clamp-on vise with you, you must have a way to clamp it to tables that are too thick for the clamp that comes with the vise. An easy way to solve this is to carry with you a small board and one or two larger "C" clamps.

The best board is shelving about 0.75-inch (19-mm) thick measuring about 4 by 6 inches (10 by 15 cm). To use, clamp the board to the table or bench using one or two "C" clamps and leave about 2 inches (5 cm) of the board extending over the edge of the table. Then clamp the "C" clamp vise to this extended part of the board and tie away.

43 PEDESTAL VS. CLAMP VISES

There are pros and cons to the kinds of vises you can choose from. Clamp-on vises are more secure and allow vertical adjustment of the vise. You must clamp them to a table that the clamp will not damage, and one that is not too thick—2 inches (5 cm) is about the maximum.

You can place pedestal vises on any table for use anywhere. You don't even need a special table or work area for tying and you can place them on surfaces other than tables or countertops.

42 ROTARY HACKLE PLIERS

To keep dry fly hackle from twisting while winding it in place on a fly, use one of the new rotary hackle pliers. You'll also find them faster to use, since they don't require rotating the hackle pliers with each turn to prevent hackle twist.

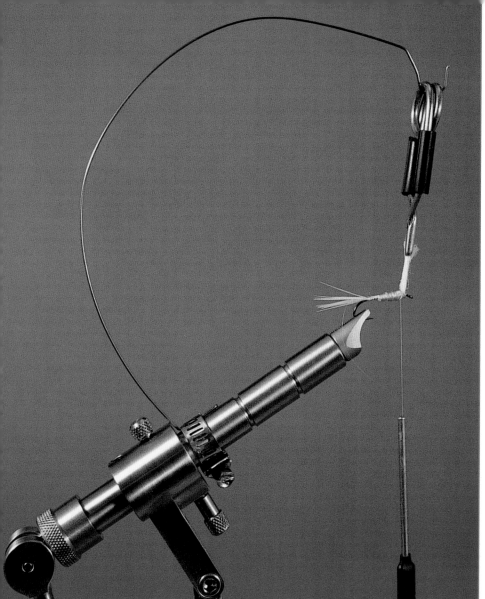

44 GALLOWS TOOL

A gallows tool is used to pull up (hang) a length of fly-tying material that you need to tie down a certain way on the hook. Anglers use them to hold up the post on dry flies when tying down parachute hackle wrapped around a post attached to the hook shank.

To make a gallows tool, get a 12- to 18-inch (30.5- to 45.7-cm) length of spring wire from a hardware store, carefully bend (wear safety glasses) a small hook in one end, and attach the other with hose clamps or cable ties to the fly-tying vise post. Then you can bend the wire down, and hold the materials with a hackle pliers, which in turn can hang from the hook in this improvised gallows tool.

45 HORIZONTAL GALLOWS TOOL

Bead-chain leeches, some 'cuda flies, long pike flies, and tandem-rigged flies require a horizontal gallows tool, or some way to hold the tail of the fly so that it does not interfere with tying the rest of the fly. To do this, set up a clamp to hold a vertical post to the left of your fly-tying vise. Run a tension spring (available from hardware or home supply stores) from the vertical post to a hook or hackle pliers.

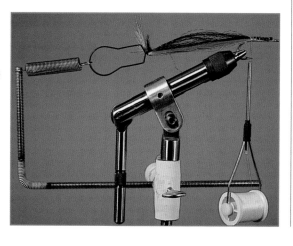

46 BEAD-CHAIN LEECHES

One easy way to hold bead-chain body out of the way when making bead-chain leeches is to bend a paper clip into a sharp "J" shape at one end and an eye (like a large hook eye) at the other end. Use the "J" to hook onto the last bead of the bead chain and attach the other end of this hook to the spring of the horizontal gallows tool. This allows holding the bead chain out of the way for tying materials to it to tie a weighted leech.

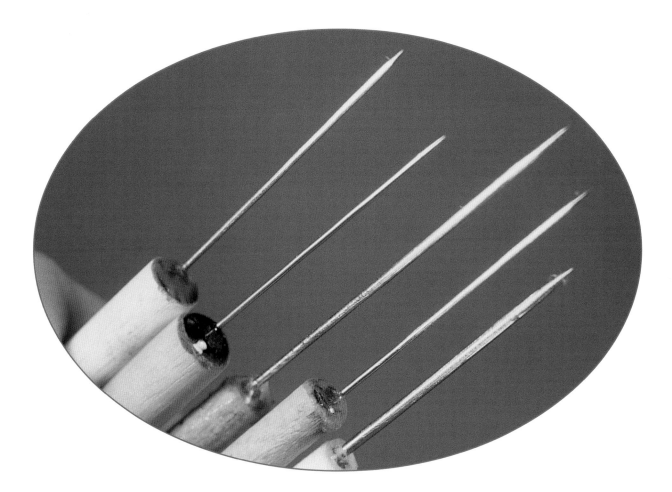

47 SIMPLE BODKIN

Get a large sewing needle (a darning needle is a good size), drill a tiny hole straight into the end of a 4-inch (10-cm) length of 1/2-inch-diameter (1.3-cm) dowel, and epoxy the eye end of the needle into the hole. Make a number of bodkins this way, since different sizes are handy for different tasks. Large, coarse bodkins are ideal for making pilot holes in foam bugs for inserting the hook; medium bodkins are best for placing head cement precisely on the head of a small fly; small bodkins are good for separating fibers in wet fly and dry fly hackle.

"When dressing dry-flies, we must always keep in mind the fish's point of view rather than our own."

Romilly Fedden
Golden Days (1919)

48 TINY BODKINS

The center veins of stripped feathers, left over from wrapping hackle or tying in dry fly wings, are ideal as tiny "bodkins" by which you can add small drops of head cement to tiny flies. Keep a bunch of these around in a container for use and dispose of them when head cement clogs them.

50 BEAD-CHAIN FLY HANGING RACKS

To make a rack for hanging flies while head cement cures or while paint on bugs dries, make a wide "U"-shaped wood bracket for a base and sides, and then string bead chain across the top, stapled to the top of the side supports. The bead chain keeps the flies from sliding together and being ruined, even if there is a little slack in the chain. Several sizes of bead chain are available, depending on the size of the fly that you need to hang. Bead chain is readily available through hardware and home supplies stores.

49 TOOL RACK

It won't be neat, but you can make a simple rack for your fly-tying tools from a scrap block of shipping foam. Use a pencil to punch holes for bodkins, bobbins, whip finishers, dubbing spinners, scissors, etc. Use a piece of pipe or tubing to cut and make blind holes for stackers, bottles of head cement, and similar items.

51 FLY DRYING RACK

Stick pins—headfirst—into a wood board (drill a hole for each pin in a row) to make a rack that allows you to hang flies by the hook eye instead of the bend. This prevents head cement from clogging up the eye of the hook.

The best way to do this is to drill tiny holes in the board, add a drop of glue to each hole, and insert the head of the pin. Bend the pins into a hook shape so that the fly head does not glue to the board holding the pins. Place the board on a stand about 6 inches (15.2 cm) high, so that the flies can hang straight down.

TOOLS & HOW TO USE THEM

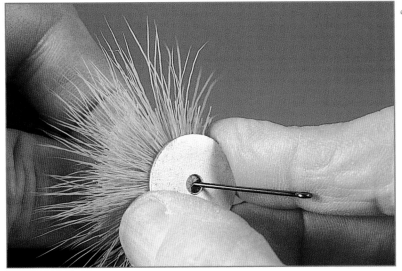

52 HAIR PACKER

A fender washer is a good tool to use as a hair packer for pushing spun deer hair when making deer-hair bass bugs. These are large-diameter washers with small holes. Most external diameters are from about 1 to 1 1/2 inches (2.5 to 3.8 cm). The inside diameter of the holes start around 1/8 inch (3 mm). Get several of the smallest sizes to fit over different-size hook eyes. These are readily available from any good hardware store.

53 ANOTHER HAIR PACKER

Another easy way to make a hair packer is to cut 3/4-inch-diameter (1.9-cm) dowels into 4-inch (10.2-cm) lengths, then drill straight into the end of the dowel. Make several, with holes ranging from about 1/16- to 1/4-inch (2- to 6-mm) diameter, to fit over the eyes of hooks on which you tie. Drill the hole deep so that you can slide it over any size hook shank. The dowel is easy to hold while pushing it over a hook eye to compact the hair on a bug.

"I carry fewer flies each year, and less gear. Each year I watch a little more, fish a little less. My expertise with a fly rod, such as it is, fails to improve much."

Christopher Camuto
A Fly Fisherman's Blue Ridge (1990)

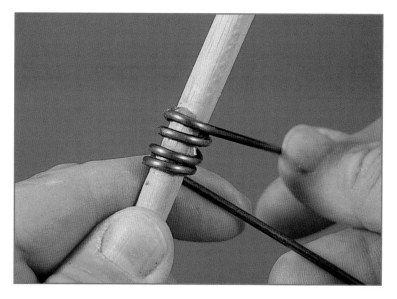

54 BOBBIN REST

Sometimes it helps to have a bobbin rest by which you can extend your thread or bobbin to the side of the vise to complete certain tying operations. You can buy these or you can make your own temporary rest with a length of coat-hanger wire. First untwist and straighten the coat hanger. Then bend one end in a spiral several times around the post of your fly-tying vise.

Remove the coat-hanger wire and bend the end of the last coil into a slightly tighter wrap that "grips" the post. Re-attach the coil to the post, with the long end of the wire at the top. Then bend this out to the side, make a second right angle vertical bend, and make any small "U" or "V" shape bends at the end with pliers to hold the thread or bobbin. Use wire cutters (wear safety glasses) to remove any excess wire.

The result is a simple, flexible rest that swings out to the side to hold your thread and bobbin. You can swing it back out of the way on the vise or remove it at any time. And the price is right.

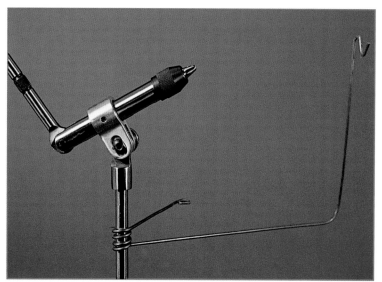

"...fishermen constitute a separate class or subrace among the inhabitants of the earth."

Grover Cleveland
(1837-1908)

55 SCISSORS PROTECTORS

Scissors protectors are available as small rubber cones into which you slip the scissors to protect them. Check with a craft or sewing supply store for these, and use them for all your fine-point scissors.

56 OTHER SCISSORS PROTECTORS

Another way to protect scissors' points is to stick them into a bottle cork when not in use.

57 PREVENTING HEAD CEMENT SPILLS

It is not uncommon to spill head cement or nail polish, ruining anything on your workbench and even the workbench finish. To prevent this, punch out a bottle-size hole in a piece of shipping or packing foam.

For a round bottle, use a spade bit to drill almost through a square block of 2 by 4 inches (5.1 by 10.2 cm), which will be 4 by 4 by 2 inches (10.2 by 10.2 by 5.1 cm) thick. This creates a hole sized to fit the bottle and holds the bottle upright to prevent spilling. The wood container also has some weight to help prevent spills.

58 ANOTHER WAY TO PREVENT SPILLS

Another way to prevent a bottle from spilling is to place it on the center of a 4- to 6-inch (10.2- to 15.2-cm) square of stiff cardboard and then use tape on the four sides to tape the bottle to the cardboard base. While you can use any tape, masking and duct tape work well for this and are easy to handle.

If you want to remove and replace the bottle from the cardboard base, do not tape to the bottle, but instead tape to a wrap of paper or cardboard around the bottle. This makes a custom-sized recess to hold the bottle securely, while allowing instant removal.

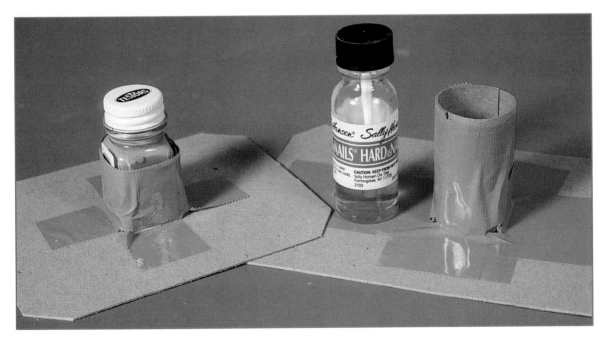

59 DUBBING TEASERS

Use a razor blade to shorten the bristles of an old toothbrush to make a teaser for fraying out dubbing and similar materials on a fly to make them look more lifelike.

Use the teaser like a comb to pull out fibers to make the fly buggy. For best results, the teaser brush should have bristles about 1/8 to 3/16 inch (3 to 4.8 cm) long.

60 ANOTHER WAY OF MAKING A DUBBING TEASER

Another way to make a dubbing teaser is to glue a small strip of the "hook" side of hook-and-loop (Velcro) fastener to half a Popsicle stick, split lengthwise. Comb the fly body with this tool so that the hook part of the hook-and-loop fastener pulls out fibers to make the fly buggy and lifelike.

61 MIXING DUBBING

An easy way to mix a large amount of dubbing material is to use two small, fine-tooth dog combs to work the material back and forth to mix different materials. Add a little of the dubbing material at a time and mix the two or more colors and materials back and forth until there seems to be a complete homogenized mix of color and fiber.

62 MARKING THREAD SPOOLS

Labels come off of thread spools, and then you don't know what size thread you have on any one bobbin. To prevent confusion, use a fine felt-tip pen to carefully write the thread size on the edge of the spool. If the edge of the spool is too narrow to write the thread size, use a series of straight marks to indicate the size in /0 sizes. Use a narrow mark for a "1" and a wide mark for "5," the same way fly anglers mark lines for their weight. Thus, three straight marks or III can be used to indicate a 3/0 thread, a wide mark and three small marks (5+3) to indicate an 8/0 thread and two wide marks (5 + 5) to indicate a 10/0 thread.

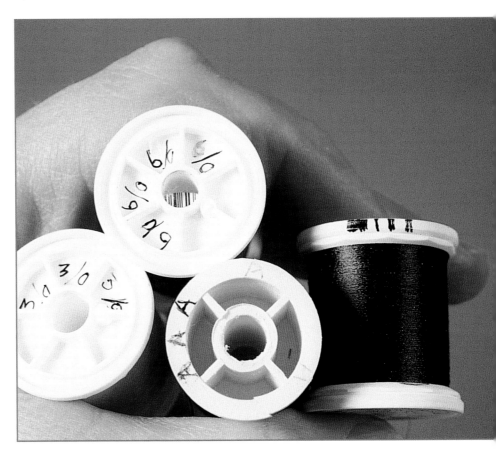

63 COMPUTER-GENERATED THREAD LABELS

Got a computer? Make a label the size of the thread spool that you are using. Set your computer to the smallest type size, and then write a number of thread sizes such as 10/0, 8/0, 6/0, 3/0, etc. Leave room between each number. Then print the numbers on a self-stick label sheet. Carefully cut out each number, stick it to the center shaft of the bobbin, and coat the label with clear head cement to protect and preserve it. Just remember that you can only use that size thread with that bobbin unless you remove the label on the shaft.

64 OTHER THREAD SPOOL MARKINGS

Another way to mark thread spools on a bobbin is to use a small self-stick label, write the size of the thread on the label with a felt-tip pen and attach the label to one arm of the bobbin holding that thread size. Just make sure that you remove the label each time to change thread spool sizes in each bobbin.

65 MARKING THREAD BOBBINS

Another way to mark the thread size on bobbins is to use a fine felt-tip pen to write the size of the thread on a small plastic washer, and then slip the washer over one arm of the bobbin before adding the thread spool.

66 BOTTLE BRUSHES

To use nail polish to seal the head or thread wraps on a fly, first trim the brush in the bottle cap. To do this, remove the brush and wipe it clean. Then use scissors to cut upward into the brush at an angle to taper and thin the brush end. Be sure to clean your scissors after doing this trick.

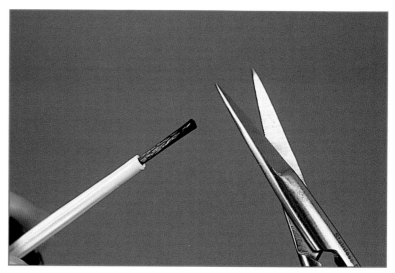

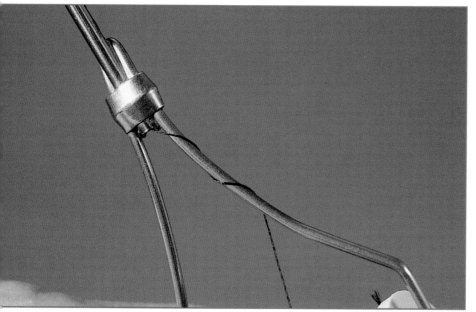

67 ADJUSTING BOBBIN TENSION

To create more resistance to thread coming off of the spool on a bobbin, run the thread once or twice around one arm of the bobbin to create more friction on the thread. Usually this works best on bobbins that have long side arms, which creates less of an angle as the thread travels from the spool to the arm and back to the center shaft.

68 BODKIN PROTECTION

To keep a bodkin from stabbing you, stick it in a small bottle cork when not in use or stick it into a foam tool rack. If your tool rack is of hard wood or plastic, glue or tape a section of foam to one side or the back to store bodkins.

69 MORE BOBBIN ADJUSTMENTS

To create more pressure to hold thread onto a bobbin without running the thread around the arm, use a rubber band or an O-ring around the two arms above the thread spool. Generally, an O-ring of about 2-inch (2.5-cm) diameter is about right, but take the bobbin and spool with you to the hardware store to check and get the right size for your bobbin.

If you use a rubber band, encircle the bobbin arms several times to get the correct tension for the thread you're using and for your tying style.

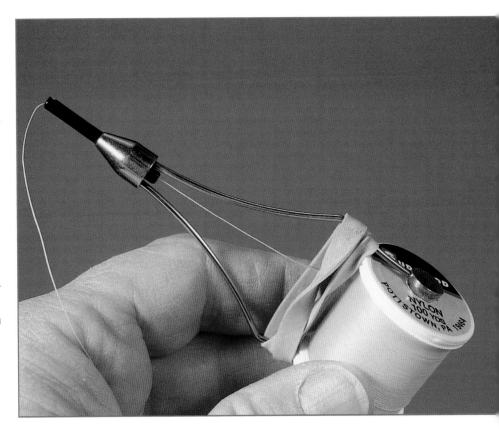

"No matter how long an angler does it, fly fishing remains an endless, delightful surprise. That's what we love about it. We can do our best to understand fish, and we can make no end of calculations about their behavior but we cannot ever take for granted that they will eat our flies. Sometimes we understand why a fish says yes or no to a hook decorated with feathers and fur or hair and tinsel; often we don't. To people who don't study a river's face to learn what is in its heart, or turn over riverbed rocks to find the life beneath them, or see the image of a mayfly in little pieces of birds and critters attached to a hook, the whole game must seem a frivolous exercise in chance. To we who enjoy this sport, the mysteries make perfect sense. We can count on being surprised. That's reason enough to go back to the water."

Art Scheck

70 OTHER USES FOR THREAD BOBBINS

You can also use a thread bobbin to hold other fly-tying products, such as brass/copper wire, lead wire, very fine yarn, fine chenille, floss, etc. This makes it easy to wind these materials onto a fly with no waste.

71 TYING SUPPLIES

Various types of racks are available for stacking dispenser boxes of dubbing, stranded materials, etc. These make it easy to have a lot of materials readily available for tying different flies, while taking up little bench space.

One main supplier of these items is Spirit River, whose products are available through fly shops and catalogs. They also make racks to hold a lot of these boxes in a vertical stack or on a rotary file system. You can also make your own racks from scrap wood or lengths of aluminum angle.

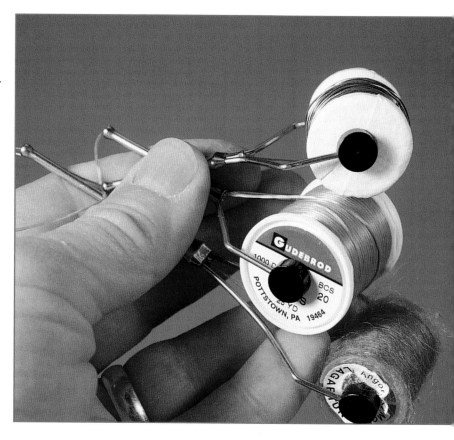

72 MIXING DUBBINGS

One way to thoroughly mix various furs and synthetic materials for dubbing is to use a mini-blender, like a coffee grinder. Beware that sometimes the fur floats up in the blender without completely mixing.

To solve this problem, make a "lid" from a plastic food container lid that fits snugly into the blender opening. Cut this plastic to size and then add a handle with a bolt and nut through an empty thread spool and a hole in the lid. Use this to push the material down to get it mixed properly. Take care that you do not overmix, which will cause knots and tangles.

73 HEAD CEMENT

Save those snap-cap lids that come on a lot of condiment bottles and jars, such as ketchup, mustard, mayonnaise, or hot sauce. Also save small bottles, such as the short and squat screw-lid spice bottles. When both are empty, match the snap-cap lids with the small jars or bottles. Clean both and use the bottles for head cement and other liquid products that you use for fly tying.

The snap-cap makes it easy to open by snapping the lid back and inserting a bodkin to remove a small drop of head cement. Don't store a lot of head cement this way, since there is still some evaporation of solvent through these caps. In time, evaporation will cause the head cement to thicken.

74 CLEANING THREAD BOBBINS

Run heavy mono through the shaft or tube of a bobbin to push out collected wax residue that accumulates when using pre-waxed thread. 50- to 100-pound mono (22.7- to 45.4-kg) works well, as do some of the sizes of the Weed Wacker–style of weed cutters.

Push the mono through, remove the wax from the end, and then remove the mono. To make a permanent tool for this, glue one end of the heavy mono into a tiny hole drilled into the end of a 4-inch (10-cm) length of 1/2- to 3/4-inch (12.7- to 19-mm) dowel. Bright-colored Weed Wacker nylon shows up distinctly on your tying bench.

75 ALTERNATE DUBBING WAX

If you are short of dubbing wax or want to try something different, use some of the warm-weather (soft) ski wax. Make sure that it is room temperature and add it to the tying thread, loop, or dubbing strand to hold the dubbing material prior to spinning it in place and then wrapping it on the hook shank.

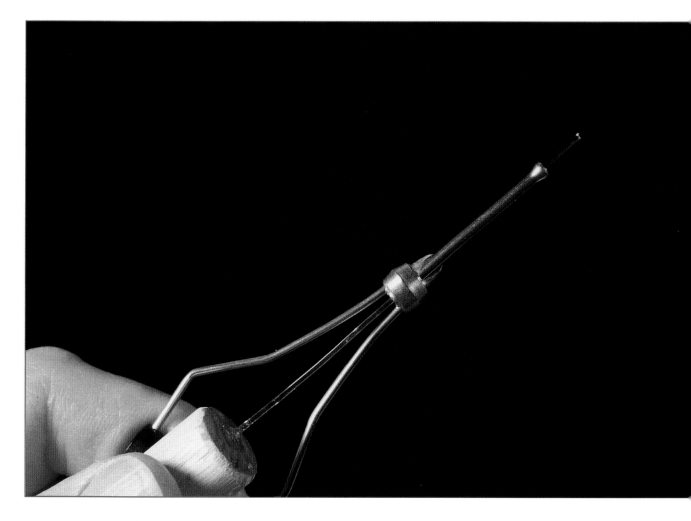

"What started as a passion, became a way of life. That way of life became a vocation, but remained a passion. It's led me to fantastic, exotic, fishing destinations around the world and offered me the chance to pioneer, innovate and most importantly, meet the people who have shaped the fly fishing world and my life."

Flip Pallot

76 PAINTING STRIPES

One way to get a striped paint pattern on a bug is to spray paint through a comb. Do this after applying a base and finish coat of paint. Vary the stripes for your bugs by using the "fine" or "coarse" teeth, or use wire cutters to cut out every other tooth of the comb.

Hold the comb about 1 inch (2.5 cm) away from the bug for best results. By holding the comb slightly away from the bug, you get a soft or "feathered" effect on the bug body.

77 MARKING MATERIALS

To create the mottled appearance of nymphs, use a light-colored body of wool, yarn, dubbing, EZ-Dub, or similar body materials, and mark as desired with an appropriate color felt-tip marker. You can get felt-tip markers in various tip sizes from art supply stores. Colors to check out include olive, dark olive, brown, tan, gray, light gray, black, dark gray, wine, and dark green.

Before trying this on a just-completed nymph, try the marker on a piece of scrap material to check how it looks and also the degree of bleeding that occurs. Often some bleeding blurs edges and makes for a more natural-looking nymph.

78 MARKING BAITFISH FLIES

Most baitfish for warm-water and saltwater species have unique markings. Yellow perch and bluegill have vertical bars; mackerel have spots and undulated markings on their backs; pinfish, striped killifish, Atlantic and chub mackerel have thin vertical bars; sardines have a longitudinal line of dots; juvenile shad have a longitudinal line of large dots; and tomcod, toadfish, and sculpin have mottled sides.

You can easily duplicate these on simple flies by using light-colored soft materials such as Aqua Fiber, Neer Hair, and similar materials. Mark these flies with felt-tip markers to add the necessary lines, dots, stripes, and mottling. Tie these flies in the appropriate background or belly color, and then use permanent felt-tip markers of the right color to add the stripes, spots, dots, and mottled dark areas.

To do this, finish tying the necessary flies, then lay each on a sheet of cardboard or white paper, and mark each by patting the side of the fly with the felt-tip marker. Next, turn the fly over and repeat with similar markings on the opposite side. Make sure that you do not soil the finished side with felt-tip marker ink on the paper that transfers to the fly. Change the paper background often to avoid this problem or work on a clean section of paper each time.

79 QUILL WING DIVIDERS

If tying traditional dry flies or wet flies where you are using barbs from duck-wing quills for the fly wings, there is an easy way to get equal wings.

Use a pair of compass dividers set to the distance for the width of the wing. For this, you want the type of divider that has two points, not one point with the other a pencil or pen nib. The two points allow separating the barbs to get the exact number for each wing.

Realize that you have to use paired quills for this, and select the same width fly wing area from each part of the two quills. Adjust the divider points to separate the quill fibers from the rest of the quill and then cut off the portion desired. If you can't find, or do not want to buy, these compass dividers, you can do the same thing with a paper clip or stiff wire, bent straight and then folded in half to place the two ends at the distance required to measure the wings.

If you change the wing size, you have to slightly re-bend the wire to reflect this change.

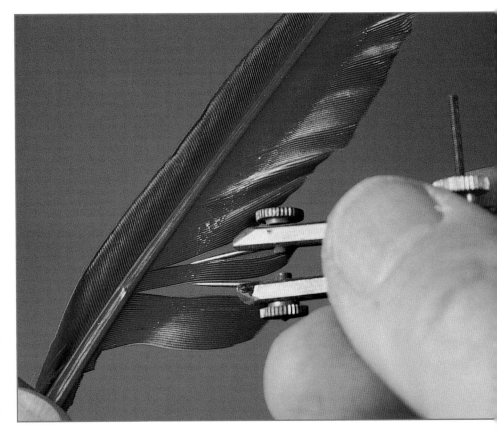

80 BODKIN CLEANER

Bodkins are great tools for all sorts of fly-tying tasks. You can clear the head cement out of a hook eye, pull matted hackle out from a thread wrap, fussy-out a body material, add cement to a fly head, pull up a whip-finish without tangles. The only problem is that cement, glue, and goo can clog bodkins. To avoid this, drill a 1/4-inch (6-mm) hole in the top of an empty film canister and fill it with steel wool. Put the cap back on and then poke the bodkin several times through the hole into the steel wool to clean it of cement.

Chapter 3

Thread: Tying On & Tying Off

81 TYING OFF WITH A HALF-HITCH TOOL

A whip finish is far better than a couple of half hitches to finish a fly. But instead of using the regular whip finish with your fingers or a tool for that purpose, try using a half-hitch tool. To complete a whip finish with a half-hitch tool, make a few thread wraps around the tool before seating it against the hook eye and sliding the thread off onto the hook shank. This makes a whip finish, even though it looks like you are just making a more complex half hitch. Because three turns of the thread around the half-hitch tool is about the maximum that you can make, two of these whip-finish variations are often best to secure the head of a fly.

82 SPOTTING DEER HAIR FOR ATTRACTIVE BASS BUGS

One way to make attractive-colored spots in a deer hair bass bug is to use different colors of deer hair.

First stack or spin the deer hair body. Then, in the area where you want a spot, fold a small bundle (cleaned and trimmed) of a contrasting color deer hair around the tying thread, hold the bundle by the two ends, and pull it into position with the tying thread.

Use this technique to make spots, stripes, variegated patterns, and even spots within larger spots. Pulling the spot in place with the thread allows you to position the spot of color exactly where you want it.

"…no man is born an artist nor an Angler."

Izaak Walton
The Compleat Angler
(1653)

83 HANDMADE HALF HITCHES

If you do not have a half-hitch tool, you can make a half hitch on a fly with your fingers. To do this, use your right index finger to maintain tension on the tying thread, then create slack in the tying thread to create a loop that you can place on the far side of the hook and pull tight to make the half hitch.

You can also do this using two fingers, starting the same way you start to make a whip finish. Once you make your loop with your two fingers by rotating your wrist to create a loop, place the loop on the far side of the hook shank, and pull tight.

84 MAKING DURABLE FLIES WITH HALF HITCHES

One way to make very durable flies is to half hitch the thread after each step in the tying process or after adding each material. This secures the material so that it is less likely to slip or come out. It also prevents a fly from coming completely apart when a toothy fish strikes.

85 CHANGING THREADS

One way to make a neat head when tying a large fly is to make the minimal wrap to hold the materials and then tie off the thread with a whip finish. Next, tie on with very fine thread, clip the excess, taper, and complete the head. Tie off carefully with a whip finish. Seal with head cement.

The thinner-diameter thread makes a neater fly head and requires fewer coats of head cement to make for a smooth, polished head.

86 TYING POINT-UP FLIES

If you are tying bonefish flies, Clouser minnows, or other flies that ride point up, be sure to put them in the vise point up for easy tying. This applies to flies that have the wing angled back toward the hook point, often with dumbbell eyes tied to the front of the hook shank for weight and stability. When adding dumbbell eyes, tie them on the top of the hook shank (opposite the point side) first, and then turn the hook over in the vise to add materials as above.

87 THREADING BOBBINS

To get thread through the bobbin shaft, insert the end of the thread into the shaft or tube opening, then suck on the tube (like sucking on a straw) to draw the thread through the bobbin. Make sure that you have enough slack thread when doing this so that you end up with the thread sticking out of the bobbin shaft.

88 WHIP FINISH

If you make a whip finish with your fingers, pulling it up can cause the loop of tying thread to twist and make a knot that will tangle the thread on the fly head.

To prevent this, make the wraps of the whip finish, and when ready to pull it up, hold the loop with a bodkin as you pull the loop tight. This controls the loop, prevents tangles, and makes it possible to pull the whip finish tight. Remove the needle tip as the thread loop pulls tight against the head.

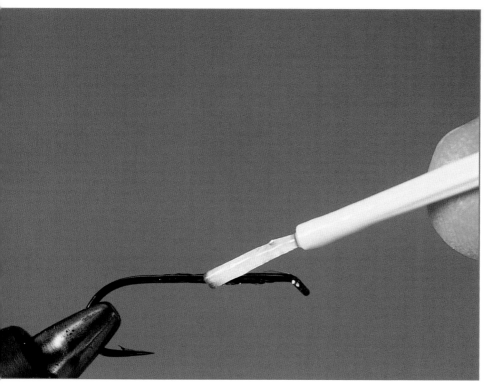

89 PREVENTING THREAD FROM SLIPPING

To make sure that the thread does not slip when tying on, put a tiny drop of head cement or nail polish on the hook where you tie down the thread. Then wrap over this wet glue base to secure the thread before cutting the excess thread. Make this only a small drop of glue, since you want the thread to absorb it all—not soak the area or become transferred to other materials, which the glue might color or stain.

90 FINE THREAD

If you're not sure what thread to use, use one that is finer than you think you need. If you break the thread when tying the first fly, you might have to go to a larger size. Thin-diameter threads are best, since they are less bulky when adding materials and make a neater fly.

91 CAPPING THREAD SPOOLS

Small plastic end caps to fit over standard thread spools are available from craft, fabric, and sewing supply stores. Use them to keep your fly-tying thread from unraveling by slipping on a cap and then catching the thread end between the plastic cap and the spool.

92 HEAVY THREAD

Use heavy thread when tying bass bugs to create enough pressure to secure the materials and make a sturdy bug. A lot of experienced flytiers use size "A" thread that is more often used for rod wrappings. Other possibilities are the various Kevlar threads and the gel-spun thread that are now available.

93 FLATTENING THREAD

One way to reduce bulk in flies is to flatten the thread. To do this, untwist the thread so that it lies flat on the hook shank. This also broadens the thread as it untwists, which is often a help in holding and securing materials.

Unfortunately, there is no industry standard as to twist direction, so you must check each manufacturer for their twist. One easy way to check this is to tie on and hang the bobbin, then wait until the bobbin starts untwisting. This is the direction you need to turn to further flatten the tying thread. If you need the thread tight in a tight twist, reverse the direction in which the thread is unwinding.

" 'How can you possibly say you just had a wonderful day? It has been windy, cold, spitting snow and all you caught were a couple of 10-inch trout.' My question was from the wife of a non-fishing friend. I tried to respond intelligently about my love of the sport. The beautiful places we fish, the wildlife we often see, the fun of just casting...but the conversation soon drifted off into other subjects. Later, I revisited the conversation and again struggled with a simple answer to her question.

Just what is the attraction? I think maybe it is that last multiple-choice test answer, 'All of the Above.' So, next time a non-fishing friend asks, I'll just change the subject."

Pete Van Gytenbeek
CEO/President, Federation of Fly Fishers

94 PUMICE STONE

Use a pumice stone to smooth your fingertips before handling fly-tying materials. This prevents snagging and tearing the working thread or other fly materials. It is particularly important when handling fine-body materials such as floss and fine threads. Many professional and commercial flytiers keep a pumice stone on their fly-tying bench to keep their fingers smooth.

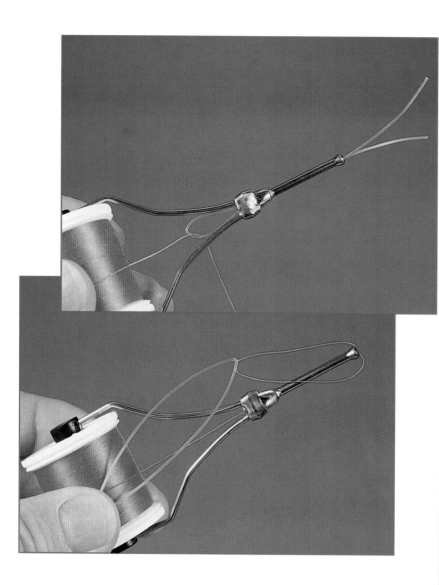

95 MORE ON THREADING BOBBINS

To pull thread through the shaft or tube of a bobbin, double a fine monofilament strand (no more than 8-pound-/3.6-kg-test), push the double end down through the end of the bobbin, run the thread end through the resulting loop, and pull the thread out through the tube or shaft.

This works like a longer version of a needle threader, which is available from sewing stores for threading needles of all types.

96 RIGHT SIZE THREAD

Too fine a thread will break when adding coarse materials on larger flies. Too coarse a thread on a small hook bulks up the fly too much and might bend the hook. Use the right size thread for the fly.

For flies 18 and smaller use size 10/0. For flies 16 to 12, use size 8/0 to 6/0; for flies 10 to 4, use size 3/0; and for flies of size 2 and larger, use size 3/0 to size A or G (Gudebrod).

These recommendations can be adjusted to your fly standards, since some flies in a given size require more thread tension (and heavier thread) than others. A prime example would be the heavy tension required to spin deer hair versus the minimal tension required to tie a thread-wrapped midge pattern.

97 WHEN A THREAD BREAKS

Every flytier has times when the thread breaks when tying a fly. Rather than throw out the fly, you can usually save it with some quick steps. First, do not touch the fly or materials. If there is a tag end to the broken thread, hold that and with the same two fingers of your left hand, grab the end of the thread still hanging from the bobbin. Then use the bobbin thread to wrap around the area where the thread broke to tie and secure any loose materials. If there is no hanging tag end of thread, just use the bobbin to wrap over the tying area to secure materials. If the thread broke in the bobbin, leave the fly alone for a moment and re-thread the bobbin.

98 SECURING WINGS

To easily tie down fly wings, hold the wing over the hook with the left hand. With the middle finger of the bobbin hand supporting the thread, bring the thread up on the near side of the fly. Then drop the thread on the far side of the fly so that the thread captures the wing. The result is a centered wing, beautifully positioned.

99 TRIMMING DEER HAIR BUGS

Instead of scissors, use a razor blade (preferably double-edge), broken in half and with the back taped for protection, to trim your deer hair bugs, muddlers, or any deer hair fly or bug. All flytiers agree that the double-edge blades are far sharper than the safer single-edge blades that are readily available in industrial packs.

100 TYING CORRECTLY

When wrapping material on a hook shank when thread is to be tied over the material (as when wrapping a yarn or chenille body after wrapping the thread forward to tie off), use the correct hand for each stage of the wrap.

Assuming right-handed tying with a right-hand-positioned vise, bring the material up and over the hook shank with the right hand, catching it with the left hand when hitting the hanging thread, and switching to the right hand again in front of the hanging working thread. The opposite of this by wrapping up and over with the left hand may hit the vise, while the right hand may hit the working thread on each wrap.

The first method is better, quicker, and surer, and with less risk of a problem.

101 BULLET-HEAD FLIES

Carrie Stevens (and later Keith Fulsher in his Thunder Creek series of patterns) first popularized bullet-head flies. To make these more lifelike, use red thread. The reason is that you can easily tie in the body and the forward-facing wing fibers with this thread hidden when you fold over and tie down the bullet head. After tying down the body and head, fold these wing fibers (usually bucktail) back over the hook. Secure these wing fibers with the red working thread to make this wrap look like gills on a small minnow, thus attracting more gamefish. When finished, complete with a whip finish and then seal the thread with head cement.

"Had all pens that go trout fishing devoted themselves to jotting down notes about why the big fish did not gobble the grasshopper, we should have lost many a page of sunshine, fresh air, and good fellowship, and reaped a crop of fireside Disko troops who thought like the fish."

William McFarland (1925)

102 "SOFT LOOPS"

Use the "soft loop" method to keep materials in proper place on the hook. To do this with a streamer wing, for example, hold the wing in place on the hook shank with your left thumb and forefinger. Bring the thread straight up to where you can pinch it between your thumb and index finger to hold it, and then bring it straight down on the back side of the fly. Pull the thread straight down to tighten the thread and secure the wing in line and on top of the hook shank.

You can use this method for adding streamer wings, dry fly wings, tails, body material, throats, or almost anything you wish on the fly hook.

103 TAPER STREAMER HEADS

When finishing a large fly such as a streamer, don't build up a big block of a head. Instead, taper the thread wrap so that it is small in the front and then tapers back to the area of the thread holding the wing in place. Doing so makes the streamer fly more fishlike in appearance and look more natural.

104 SPIN DEER HAIR OVER A THREAD-WRAPPED SHANK

Most experts agree that spinning (flaring) deer or other body hair around a hook shank to make bass bugs is easier to do over a thread-wrapped body. There is less of a tendency for the hair and thread to slip than there would be on a bare hook shank.

Wrap the thread forward neatly around the hook shank, a little at a time, as you work on the bug body. Then wrap the thread back from the front to completely cover the hook shank before beginning to spin the deer hair.

105 GAP CLEARANCE WITH BASS BUGS

When making deer hair bass bugs, place the hook shank in the body as close to the belly as you can to maintain a wide hook gap. This is necessary for sure hooking of any fish.

"There is no taking trout in dry britches."

Cervantes

Don Quixote (1605)

106 MAKING A WHIP FINISH

To make a whip finish with your fingers, place your left thumbnail
on the hook at the point where you want the whip finish to seat.
That way you can control the exact position of the whip finish so as
to not mat hackle or disfigure the head. You do this by allowing the
thread on each wrap to slide against your thumbnail and seat
against the head as you wrap. This prevents the thread from
encroaching on the back part of the wing. Wrap the working part of
the thread around the head and over the standing part of thread
before pulling the loop and whip finish tight.

Chapter 4

Handling Hooks & Making Weed Guards

107 STORING SMALL HOOKS

It is best to keep small hooks (size 16 and smaller) in their original container or in a pill-box with a tight-fitting lid to prevent loss or mix-up. You can also keep very small hooks in a labeled 35mm film canister. Just be careful not to spill the hook contents when opening the snap lids of these containers.

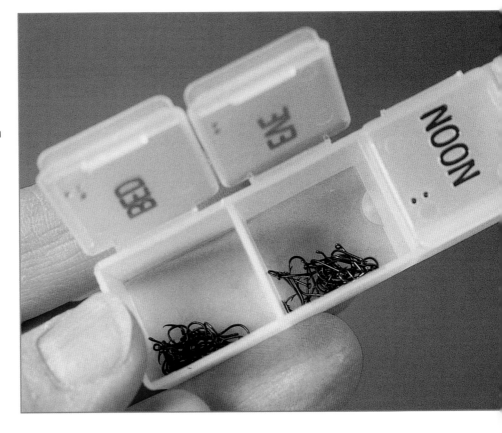

108 STRAIGHT-EYE HOOKS

If tying large flies, such as those for barracuda or pike that are attached to the leader with a braided wire bite tippet, you must use a straight-eye hook for the fly to work properly in the water. For best results, use a figure-eight knot for attaching braided wire to the hook. The straight-eye hooks keep the fly working in a straight line, thus appearing natural, rather than working at an up or down angle as would occur with a turned-up or turned-down eye hook.

109 TURLE KNOT HOOK CHOICES

If you use a Turle knot to tie on flies when fishing, you must tie all of your flies on a turned-up or turned-down eye hook. Otherwise, the knot will not work, as the mono tippet will be at an angle to the hook shank.

This is only true for the Turle knot. You can tie all other knots, such as the improved clinch knot and palomar knot, using a hook with any type of eye.

110 CORROSION-RESISTANT HOOKS

If tying saltwater flies, it is best to tie only on stainless steel, tin, or other hooks with finishes designed to resist the corrosive effects of saltwater. Most hook companies now design hooks for saltwater use, so you should be able to find regular, long shank, circle, and specialty hooks made of materials to resist corrosion.

"As the old fisherman remarked after explaining the various ways to attach a frog to a hook, it's all the same to the frog."

Paul Schullery
Mountain Time (1984)

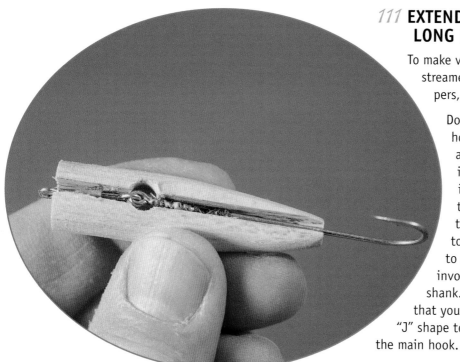

111 EXTENDING HOOKS FOR LONG POPPERS

To make very long flies for some streamers and long pencil poppers, extend the hook shank.

Do this by using a separate hook, cutting off the bend and point, and then bending the shank at the end into a "J" loop to fit into the main hook eye. Clamp this with pliers to secure it to the main hook. Make sure to use safety glasses in steps involving cutting the hook shank. Also, use soft wire hooks that you can bend into a sharp "J" shape to hook onto the eye of the main hook.

One way to soften the hook wire for bending is to touch it to a propane flame until it is red hot to remove the temper. Bend it with pliers while still hot.

112 ANOTHER HOOK EXTENSION METHOD

Another way to extend hook shank length for poppers is to add a connector link. These are available in regular tackle shops and consist of an extended chain-like link with a sliding sleeve to secure the link. These are easy to put on and glue into a popper body or tie with the rest of the fly. You can add just one to a hook or several in a "chain" to get additional length.

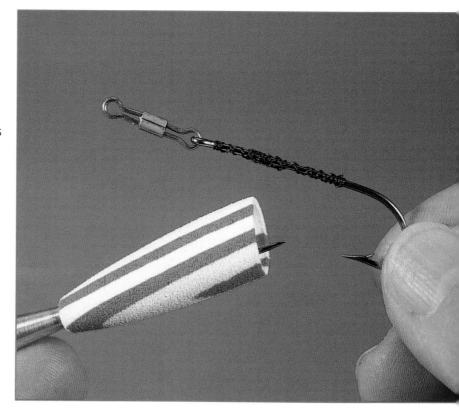

HANDLING HOOKS & MAKING WEED GUARDS

113 CHECKING FLY HOOKS FOR SHARPNESS

Most fly hooks are sharp as they come out of the box. However, it does help to check each hook for sharpness by touching the point to your thumbnail to see if it catches. If it does, it is sharp; if not, sharpen it.

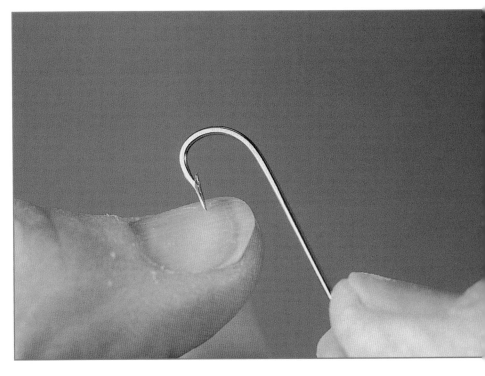

To sharpen fly hooks, place the fly in the vise, then use a very fine hook hone or sharpening file on the hook. Sharpen by running the sharpening instrument at an angle over the point, running the file between the point and hook shank. Do this at an angle, touching both the point and the barb. Then lightly touch the outside of the hook point to triangulate the hook.

You cannot do this if using circle hooks. For sharpening them, use a hook hone with a groove in it and run the hook point in the sharpening groove along the outside of the hook.

114 OPEN HOOK GAPS

To make a fly hook fish easier, use pliers to slightly open the hook gap. Do this before tying the fly, so that if the hook breaks, you will not have ruined the fly. Make this change very slight; you want to increase the gap for surer hooking, not open the hook to the point where you might lose a fish.

115 BENDING HOOK BARBS

There are two ways to bend down the barb of a hook. One is to hold the pliers at a right angle to the hook shank and bend the barb down. The second way is to hold the pliers jaws parallel to the hook point and bend. The second way is usually best, since it lessens the possibility of the hook breaking or bending.

116 REMOVING HOOK BARBS

One way to remove the barb from a fly hook to make a barbless hook or for adding a bead is to use a fine file or hook hone to file off the barb.

To do this, place the fly hook in a vise and hold the hook by the "heel" (the bend of the hook) with the point and barb protruding from the vise. Then use a fine file or diamond-dust hook hone to file down the barb. This takes longer than using pliers to bend down the barb, but is safer since there is less likelihood that the point will break.

Do this before tying the fly and consider preparing a number of hooks this way at once so that they are ready for tying later.

117 SNELLING TANDEM FLY HOOKS

One easy way to add a rear hook to a main hook to make a tandem fly is to snell the rear hook, using heavy mono for durability. Snelling is like a nail knot on the hook shank.

You can then secure the mono to the front hook by laying it alongside of the hook shank and wrapping tightly with the tying thread.

One way to keep the mono from slipping out is to use a flame to make a melted ball at the end that can't slide under the wrapped shank. If your hook has a large eye,

you can also run the mono along the hook shank, up through and over the eye, and back parallel to the hook shank. Then wrap over both of these strands of mono with the tying thread. Since you run the mono through the hook eye, there is no way that the two hooks can pull apart. Tie the fly after making this hook connection to the rear-tied fly.

118 CIRCLE HOOKS

Try tying some of your larger flies for saltwater and warm-water fishing on circle hooks. These are now available for fly tying in both standard and long shank lengths, and are ideal for catch-and-release fishing. Usually when fishing with these, the fly ends up in the corner of the mouth of the fish, and is more likely to result in a positive strike and solid hooking, along with easy unhooking.

"We wish to reproduce as nearly as possible the effect of the insect as it floats upon the stream; to deceive trout that have had enough experience of flies and of fishermen to make them a bit shy and crafty."

Theodore Gordon (1914)

119 THE RIGHT HOOK FOR SNELLING FLIES

If you are snelling a rear hook to make a tandem rig and plan to run the mono through the hook eye, you must use a hook with a turned-up or turned-down eye. (On the forward hook, you can use a turned-up eye, turned-down eye, or the commonly available straight ball eye.)

You can snell also to a straight eye hook without running the mono through the eye, since the eye serves as a "stopper" to prevent the mono from coming loose. To do this, lay the mono alongside the hook shank and eye as you snell mono to the hook.

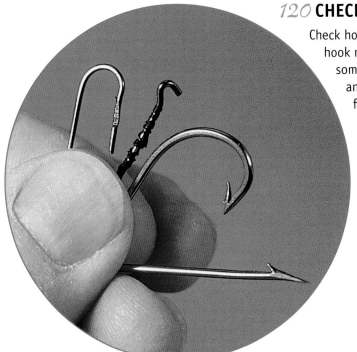

120 CHECKING FOR HOOK FLAWS

Check hooks for flaws before tying. While modern hook manufacturers have strict quality controls, sometimes a bad hook does sneak through and end up in a box. Though uncommon, flaws can include bent shanks, poor or bent points, damaged barbs, and incomplete eyes. You certainly want to discover any flaws before tying a fly on that particular hook.

121 MAKING FIXED TANDEM RIGS

You can make a hook with a fixed tandem rig by wrapping a hook, point up, to the main hook on which you tie the fly. With the main hook in the fly-tying vise, first tie on with the tying thread. Then place the second hook on top of the first with the point up. Wrap over the two hook shanks with the tying thread, spiral wrap all along the shank, and then tightly wrap the hook shank.

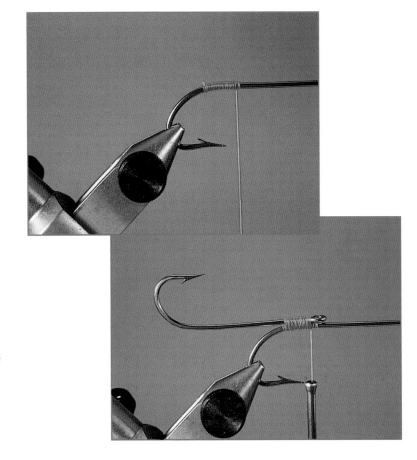

Seal with head cement or five-minute epoxy before continuing and finishing the fly. Or use shrink tubing to fasten the two hook shanks together. Then wrap the bound hooks with heavy tying thread to make sure that they will not come apart.

First make sure that such tandem or double-hook flies are legal in your area.

122 PREVENTING CUT THREAD

If you sometimes cut your thread on the point of the hook protruding from the jaws of the vise, consider clamping the hook to hide the point in the vise jaws. This way, the thread will only slide over the smooth and polished vise jaws, preventing thread breaks.

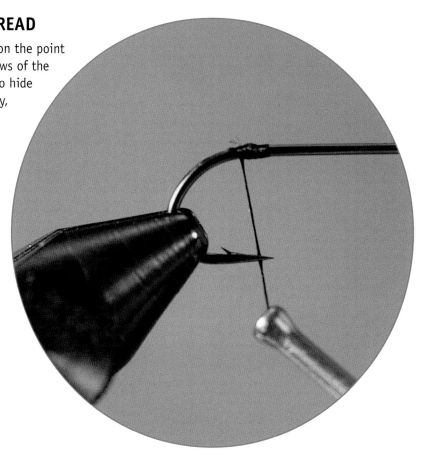

123 STORING THREAD SPOOLS

An easy way to store thread spools is on a thread spool rack sold in craft and sewing stores. These hold up to about 40 spools in a wood rack, which you can hang on the wall or prop easel-like on the fly-tying bench. You can also store other spooled materials, such as spools of wire, lead wire, braided materials, etc.

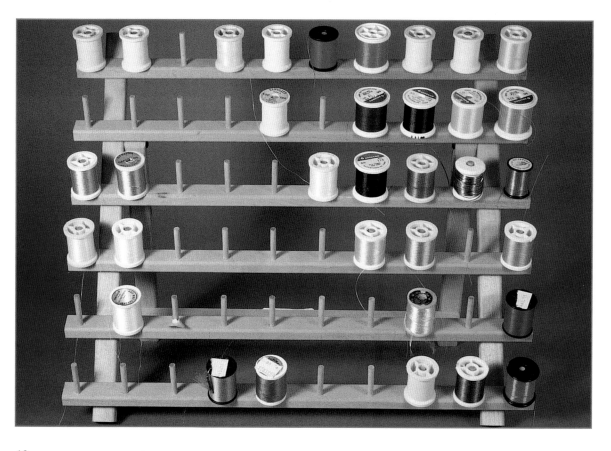

124 WEIGHTING HOOKS WITH LEAD WIRE

One of the best ways to weight a hook is to wrap lead or non-lead wire around the hook shank. You can also control the sink pattern of the fly by tying the lead along the entire shank (sinks evenly), at the rear (sinks tail first), or in back of the hook eye (sinks head first).

Of these three methods, usually the head-weighted method is best, since on a twitch retrieve, the fly gets jerked up and then falls down, creating more action and a lifelike look.

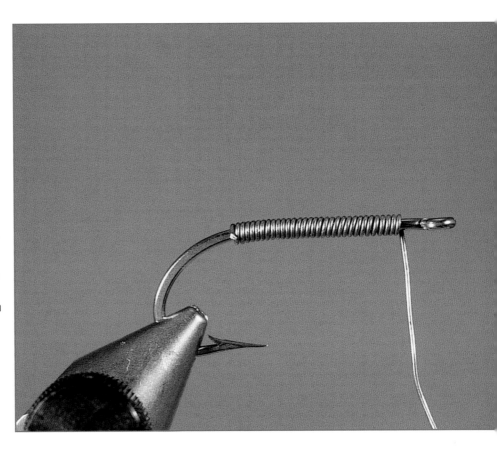

125 CONTROLLING FLY SINK RATE

You can control the sink rate of a fly with a wrapped lead or non-lead underbody by using different-size wire. Lead wire, for example, comes in sizes from 0.010- to 0.035-inch (0.254- to 0.889-mm) diameter. This is also important for adjusting the weight and size of the lead wire to the size of the hook.

"Then do you mean that I have to go on catching these damned two-and-a-half pounders at this corner forever and ever?'

The keeper nodded.

'Hell!' said Mr. Castwell.

'Yes,' said his keeper."

G.E.M. Skues
"Mr. Theodore Castwell"
Sidelines, Sidelights, and Reflections
(1947)

126 ANOTHER WAY TO ADD NON-LEAD WIRE

If adding non-lead wire to a fly hook by tying it parallel with the hook shank, it is often best to use one length or three lengths, with the three lengths spread evenly around the hookshank diameter.

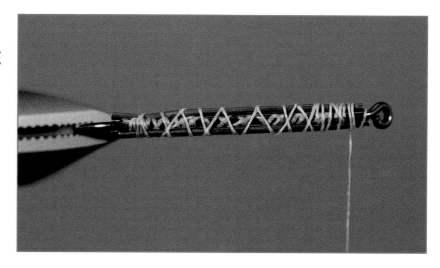

Two lengths, often described as best tied on each side of the hook, are difficult to keep in place and often loosen to slide around the hook shank. If you wish to tie in two parallel lengths of lead wire, one on each side of the hook shank, it is best to do this over a shank wrapped with a layer of thread. This tends to keep the lead from slipping. Add a drop of glue to the wrapped shank to help keep the lead or non-lead wire in place as you wrap it to the hook shank.

127 HOOK STORAGE SYSTEMS

Use a system to store your hooks. Some flytiers store hooks by size, regardless of type; others separate hooks by type (scud, shrimp, nymph, streamer, wet fly, dry fly, stainless-steel saltwater, etc.). Pick the system that works best for you so that you can find hooks easily.

One way to separate hooks is to use one of the small many-drawer compartments, such as those sold for storing nuts and bolts. You can label each drawer by size, brand, and type of hook. Storage racks are available from general and hardware stores in a variety of sizes and numbers of compartments. You can get these with anywhere from about a dozen to four dozen compartments.

128 MAKING FLAT NYMPH BODIES

Many nymphal forms of insects have flat bodies, the better to survive in fast currents. One way to make a flat body for a nymph pattern is to first wrap the hook shank with lead wire and then use pliers to flatten the lead wrap. Continue to tie the fly, following other tips for using lead and creating lifelike flies. For these nymph patterns, the lead helps to sink the fly to where the trout are located, and the shape helps to fool the trout into thinking the fly is a live insect—a typical flat-bodied nymph.

129 POPPER HOOK

Some popper hooks come in both regular- and long-shank styles. For almost all fishing, you get more and deeper strikes by using the long-shank popper hooks. This allows more of the hook point to extend in back of the bug and keeps the bug at a more pronounced angle in the water for better hooking. It also allows more room when tying on tails and collars.

130 PICKING THE RIGHT SIZE WIRE

One simple way to pick the right size lead or non-lead wire for your fly is to choose wire that approximates the hook diameter. You can do this by sight or feel, with the best way holding the wire against the shank of the chosen hook to see if both feel about the same diameter. While hooks of various model numbers within a manufacturer's line and definitely between manufacturers do vary, a rough chart that you might use follows:

LEAD WIRE DIAMETER APPROX.	HOOK SIZE STANDARD HOOKS
0.010 inch/0.254 mm	16 and smaller
0.015 inch/0.381 mm	14
0.020 inch/0.508 mm	10
	12
0.025 inch/0.635 mm	8
0.030 inch/0.762 mm	6
	4
0.035 inch/0.889 mm	2 and larger

131 RAMPING

Make a "ramp" of thread when tying in a wrap of non-lead wire to a hook shank for weight. To make a smoothly tapered body on a fly tied with wraps of wire around the hook shank, use the tying thread first to crisscross and spiral wrap over the lead wrap to help secure it. Then use the tying thread at each end of the wrapped lead wire to make a tapered "ramp." This allows you to wrap the body material over the lead wire without the over-body making a "jump" or creating a gap as it goes from the hook shank to the wire wrap.

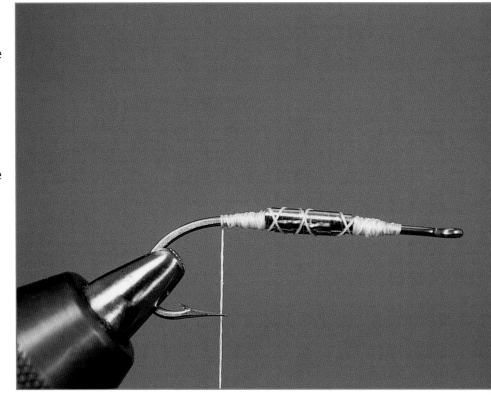

132 ADDING MONO-LOOP WEED GUARDS

When adding a mono-loop weed guard, tie the weed guard in at the tail of the fly before adding any materials. To make the weed guard a little stiffer, wrap tight turns of thread around the hook shank and mono down on the bend of the hook. Cover about half of the hook bend. Then bring the thread back up to the straight part of the hook shank and tie the rest of the fly before tying off and finishing the weed guard.

133 COMPLETING MONO WEED GUARDS

When wrapping down the end of mono to complete a mono weed guard, position the mono on the hook, make a few wraps, and then pull the weed guard forward to clip the excess mono. Once you clip the mono, use a match or lighter to form a ball on the end. Then pull the mono back into position on the fly and continue wrapping and tying off. The ball on the end of the mono prevents the weed guard from pulling free.

134 WIRE WEED GUARDS: ONE

For durable weed guards, use plastic-coated braided wire, bent into a slight "Z" or "S" shape, tied in at the head of the fly and then bent down to protect the hook point. For best results, use 30-pound-test (13.6-kg) for flies size 2 and smaller, and 40-pound-test (18.1-kg) for flies size 1 and larger.

If you are fishing really heavy weeds, use a double-point (prong) weed guard.
Use epoxy when seating this weed guard so that it will not come loose.

135 WIRE WEED GUARDS: TWO

One way to make a wire weed guard on a fly is to use light monel (single strand) wire such as 12-pound-test (5.4-kg), fold it in half, and then bend a slight angle into the folded end. If you are used to trolling wire sizes, use size 5 for flies size 1/0 and smaller and use size 7 for flies 2/0 and larger. Tie this folded end to the hook under the fly head, secure tightly, and then finish the fly. Use wire cutters (wear safety glasses) to trim the two ends of the wire to protect and extend on either side of the hook point.

136 FINISHING MONO-LOOP WEED GUARDS

To finish a mono-loop weed guard after tying the rest of the fly, position the loop of mono so that it is big enough to protect the hook point without being so big as to be unwieldy. Note that you might be positioning or changing the loop position depending upon how you tie it down, so take care that you configure the loop for the final position that it makes on the completed fly.

137 DOUBLE MONO WEED GUARDS

To get more protection for a fly when fishing in heavy weeds or through snags, use a double mono weed guard. The steps for this are identical as when tying a single-mono-loop weed guard, except that you start with two strands of mono. Make sure that both mono loops are identical and angled slightly to the side of the hook point to best protect it.

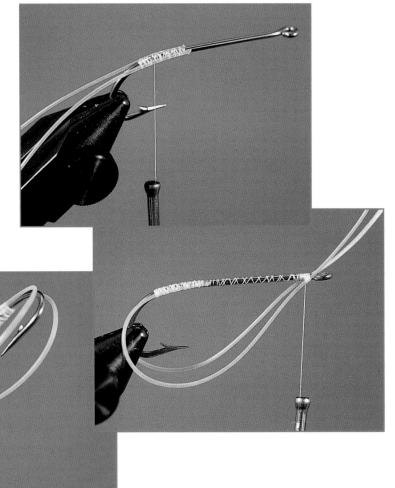

138 FITTING BEADS TO HOOKS

If a metal bead does not quite fit onto a forged shank hook, you can often make it fit. To do this, place the bead in a shop vise and just barely tighten the vise so that the bead slightly flattens to make the hole oval. Then slip the bead onto the hook point after bending down the barb. Since you have flattened the bead, you can adjust it so that the flat hole lines up with the forged shank and bend of the hook to slide around the bend easily. Then move the bead up to the eye of the hook and tie in place with working thread.

139 WEIGHTED-WIRE NYMPHS

Tie simple, weighted nymph imitations with a wrap of brass or copper wire, and a head of peacock herl. These are very similar to the so-called Brassie patterns used to get deep to trout.

On some waters prohibiting lead, flies with brass wire may not be legal. Brass does contain small amounts of lead, so check before fishing.

"Many ask, 'Why do you fish?' I've heard the standard answers: 'It's the challenge.' 'It's the wonderful destinations.' 'It's the people you meet.' 'It's the serenity.' I've thought about it a bunch, and for me it's meant many things, over the years, but these days, it's just LEAVING THE DOCK."

Flip Pallot

140 IDENTIFYING WEIGHTED FLIES

You can't tell by looking at a fly whether or not it is weighted. One way to mark flies to indicate whether they are weighted is to use different head colors.

You could tie non-weighted flies with white thread and weighted flies with black thread. You can even go further by marking non-weighted, lightly weighted, and heavily weighted flies by using three different colors of thread. White, red, and black heads are good examples.

You can also indicate fully-weighted, rear-weighted, and front-weighted flies the same way. Red, orange, and pink are favorite colors for this system. Just don't make too complicated a system that you have trouble remembering.

141 FLY-TYING WIRE SOURCES

Electronics stores are a good source of inexpensive wire for fly tying. Try to buy the least amount of wire possible, or get an assorted pack of wire sizes and colors. Often very fine wire is best for tying bodies or ribbing.

142 ADDING BEADS AND CONES TO FLY HOOKS

When adding beads or cone heads to a fly, use hooks with a symmetrical round bend, sometimes known as a Perfect Bend. This prevents a sharp radius of the bend as might occur with an Aberdeen, O'Shaughnessy, Limerick, or other similar fly hook styles from stopping or restricting the bead.

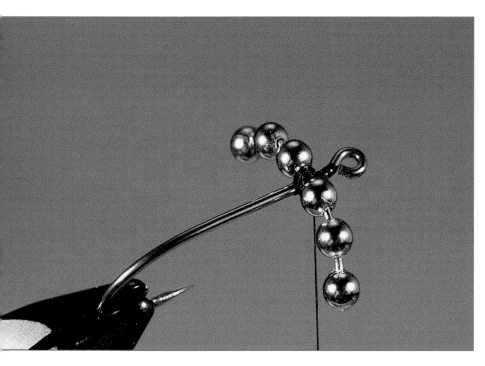

143 MAKING BEAD CHAIN EYES

To make bead chain eyes with more weight, action, and flash, use four or six beads, which places two to three eyes on each side of the fly. These also help the fly to stay upright with the point up when the fly scoots along the bottom.

Another advantage is that the two or three beads on each side of the fly add both flash and rattle noise as they move around.

144 WEIGHTING FLIES

Bead chain makes ideal eyes for flies, particularly when you want a large eye without the weight of lead or non-lead dumbbell or hourglass eyes. Bead chain is available from hardware stores or home supply stores, and comes in several sizes in both brass and bright nickel. Some fly shops also carry this, where it is also available in several sizes of stainless steel for saltwater flies.

To use, cut off two of the beads with wire cutters (use safety glasses). Wrap them into the head of the fly with thread as you would dumbbell or hour-glass eyes, wrapping around the wire joint between the two beads as you hold the bead chain eyes crosswise on the hook shank.

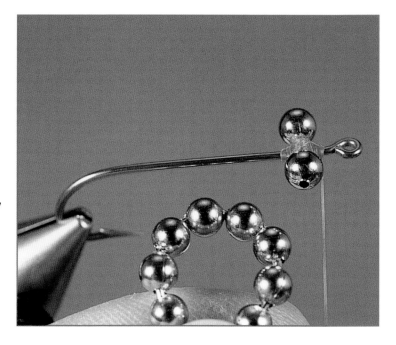

145 WEIGHTING METAL AND OTHER BEADS

You can make metal bead heads even heavier by a simple trick. Most metal beads have a tapered hole, with the larger open end of the hole designed to fit toward the rear of the fly and the small hole to fit against the hook eye. Slide the bead onto the hook shank and around to the hook eye. Make a wrap of one or two turns of lead or non-lead wire around the hook shank in back of the bead. Then push the wrap of lead wire forward and into the hole to hide it. Use pliers to push the lead forward if necessary. Tie on the thread in back of the bead and wrap around the hook shank in back of the bead and lead wire to keep the lead wrap in place.

You can do this with any size fly, since lead and non-lead wire comes in 0.010- to 0.035-inch (0.254- to 0.889-mm) diameters.

146 WEIGHTING LEECHES

Tie leech patterns with a weight, dumbbell eye, or hourglass eye in the front, since they are retrieved in an up/down fashion, which is close to the swimming action of a real leech.

To get the fly to swim this way, use slight twitches to cause it to fall on the pause, jerking it back up with each twitch.

147 ADDING TUNGSTEN TO FLY HEADS FOR WEIGHT

To add weight to the head of a fly, add tungsten or lead powder to the head sealer. This works best with the thicker epoxy coatings on large flies, but you can also add it to head cement and fingernail polish. Lead or tungsten powder is available in golf shops. Some fly-tying stores (at this writing) are starting to sell it also.

To add it to epoxy, first squeeze out equal parts of the resin and hardener and then add the powder to one of these two parts. When you have stirred the weighted powder into one part, mix the two parts completely and add to the fly. Stir frequently to keep the tungsten powder suspended in the fluid.

You can do the same thing by adding the powder to a small puddle of head cement or clear nail polish. Because of the added weight of this material, place the fly on a rotator for curing.

"Skill at the riverside, or at the fly-table, never came, nor ever will come to us by any road than that of practice."

George M. Kelson
The Salmon Fly (1895)

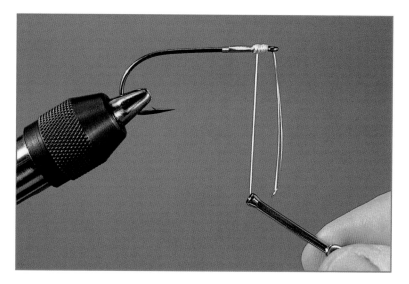

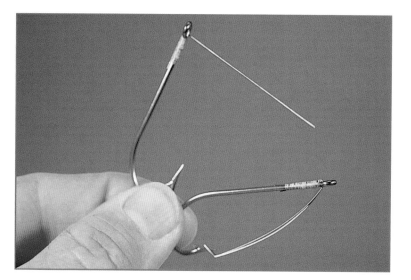

148 SINGLE-STRAND WEED GUARDS

To make a single-strand weed guard from a length of wire, clip the wire about one-and-a-half times the length between the eye of the hook and the hook point, then fold at a right angle about 1/8 inch (3 mm) from the end of the wire. Tie this short length on the underside of the hook, then finish the fly. (One reason for folding the wire into a right angle is to gives you room for additional wraps to finish tying the fly.)

Then, with the fly finished, bend the wire back to almost touch the point of the hook. Make a final bend with pliers to bend the wire just under the hook point and use wire cutters (wear safety glasses) to cut this end to about 1/8 inch (3 mm). The result is a simple "skid" type of weed guard to protect the hook point. You can also do this with a doubled wire to "capture" the hook point with the folded wire.

149 THICK HACKLE FOR A WEED GUARD

For a "suggestion" of a weed guard on a fly, tie a thicker-than-normal hackle. The thicker hackle (whether beard or collar style) serves as a weed guard to shield the hook point. Use long hackle that protects the point and wrap thread around the beard to direct most of the hackle to protect the point. You can also tie in material such as fur or calf tail to stiffen the hackle to make it a stiffer weed guard.

"Between them, the old men must have created hundreds of trout flies, insect mutants as bizarre and seductive as any ever to drop from a fly tier's vise. With perhaps two exceptions, none of their titillating offerings ever stirred a trout's interest, a fact that didn't bother them at all."

Harry Middleton
The Earth Is Enough (1989)

HANDLING HOOKS & MAKING WEED GUARDS

150 MONO SIZE FOR WEED GUARDS

The best size mono for tying mono-loop weed guards is about 20-pound-test (9.1-kg) for most flies (about size 1 through 2/0). Go as light as 12-pound-test (5.4-kg) for flies size 2 and smaller, and go as heavy as 30-pound-test (13.6-kg) for flies size 3/0 and larger.

A good guide to making a mono weed guard is to use regular fishing monofilament that is about half the diameter as that of the hook shank. This ensures the right stiffness and protection, without it being too stiff to prevent strikes or too weak and collapsing to catch a weed. Below is a rough guide. Realize that the wire diameters of hooks vary with model, manufacturer, and style of hook (2X fine for dry flies; 3X stout for nymphs). Mono diameters for a given pound-test also vary with the manufacturer and type of mono. Use the chart below as a starting point for experimentation and develop a system for your tying.

HOOK SIZE	HOOK DIAMETER	MONO POUND-TEST
14	approx. 0.0177 inch/0.45 mm	6 (approx. 0.009 inch/0.228 mm 2X)
12	approx. 0.020 inch/0.508 mm	8 (approx. 0.010 inch/0.254 mm 1X)
10	approx. 0.0225 inch/0.571 mm	10 (approx. 0.0120 inch/0.305 0X)
8	approx. 0.025 inch/0.635 mm	12 (approx. 0.013 inch/0.330 mm)
6	approx. 0.028 inch/0.711 mm	15 (approx. 0.015 inch/0.381 mm)
4	approx. 0.033 inch/0.838 mm	15 (approx. 0.015 inch/0.381 mm)
2	approx. 0.035 inch/0.889 mm	15 (approx. 0.015 inch/0.381 mm)
1 and larger	approx. 0.040 inch/1.016 mm	20 (0.018 inch/0.457 mm)
		30 (0.026 inch/0.660 mm)

151 MAKING BONEFISH FLIES SNAGPROOF

Mix in a few strands of monofilament with the wing of a bonefish fly to make it even more snag resistant. These flies, tied point up with the wing flared over the hook point, are semi-snagproof anyway. By adding a little mono, or a single strand of 20-pound-mono (9.1-kg) hidden and veiled in the regular materials wing, you can make them completely snagproof while hiding the mono weed guard.

152 BRUSH GUARD MONO WEED GUARDS

To make a stiff weed guard for a large fly, use a few strands of monofilament line, bundled to make a brush-style weed guard. Use light, 8- to 12-pound-test (3.6- to 5.4-kg) mono for flies to size 2; and use 12- to 20-pound-test (5.4- to 9.1-kg) for larger flies. If possible, pick stiff mono rather than limp, cold-water styles.

Clip a few strands, arrange them into a small bundle, even the ends, and then fold the ends into a right angle with a pair of needle-nose pliers. Then tie in the short end under the head of the fly, clip any excess, and finish the head. Trim the free ends of the nylon with scissors short enough to reduce visibility, but long enough to protect the hook point.

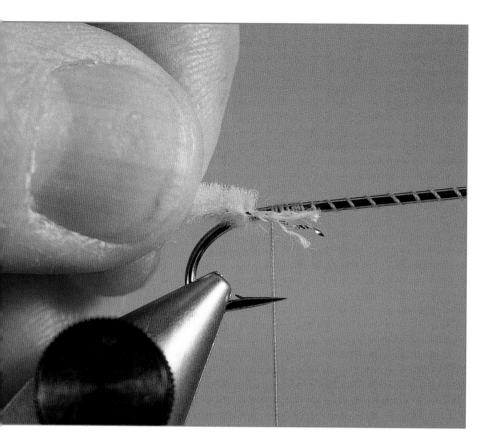

153 CHENILLE TYING TIPS

If you do not want to lay down a length of chenille along the hook shank when tying on at the rear of the hook to prevent lumps, use your thumbnail and index fingernail to pull fibers from the tag end. This exposes the thin core of two or three threads that have little bulk and are easy to tie down. Use these threads to tie down chenille to prevent any bulk buildup that would mar the appearance of the finished fly.

154 MAKING WORM FLIES

It is easy to make a bass fly that resembles the plastic worm used by spinning and casting bass anglers. To do this, use cactus chenille. Tie a length (about three times the length of the worm desired) to the rear of the hook shank. Then hold the cactus chenille at about two-thirds the length from the hook and twist in the same direction that the material was twisted to create the chenille.

After a few turns, hold a bodkin in the middle of this twisted length and fold the chenille over on itself to tie down at the rear of the hook shank. Release the bodkin and the cactus chenille will twist on itself. Tie down well and wrap the thread forward. Use the remainder of the cactus chenille to wrap around the hook shank and tie off at the head.

HANDLING HOOKS & MAKING WEED GUARDS

155 FOAM BEETLE BODIES

The best way to get a natural-looking beetle body of foam is to tie in a short length of flat foam at the rear of the hook shank with the foam facing the rear. Then wrap the thread forward, fold the foam over, and tie down with the thread. Add legs or fold over previously wrapped legs to complete this simple bug.

Make segments wrapping the thread forward to the point where you want the segmentation, then fold over the foam and segment the body at that point with the tying thread. Tie off with a whip finish at the head of the fly.

156 MAKING TAPERED WORM ENDS

To make a tapered end to a worm fly, such as a San Juan worm, use a lighter or butane grill starter to lightly burn/melt the end of the chenille. Then carefully use your fingers to twist and taper it. The chenille is hot, but should not burn you. By doing this and creating a taper in the ends of the worm, you make it more life-like and natural.

157 TYING WORM FLIES WITH CHENILLE

When tying worm flies where the chenille ends are exposed, make sure that you use Ultra Chenille, Vernille, or similar products that will not fray like standard tying chenille. This is important with small flies, such as the popular San Juan worm for trout fishing.

158 MAKING A CADDIS CASE NYMPH

Make a simple caddis imitation by wrapping a few turns of peacock herl onto a hook directly behind the eye and tying off. Coat the fly with a waterproof glue (five-minute epoxy, Ultra Flex, Duco, etc.) and roll the result in sand. Then use your fingers to roll the sand around the hook to make it like a mini sandy cigar. The result is a fly that imitates the caddis sand cases, with the peacock herl suggesting the head of the larvae peeking out of the case. These sink well, fish great, and are easy to make. If not illegal, bring home some sand from places you trout fish to duplicate the cases these insects make.

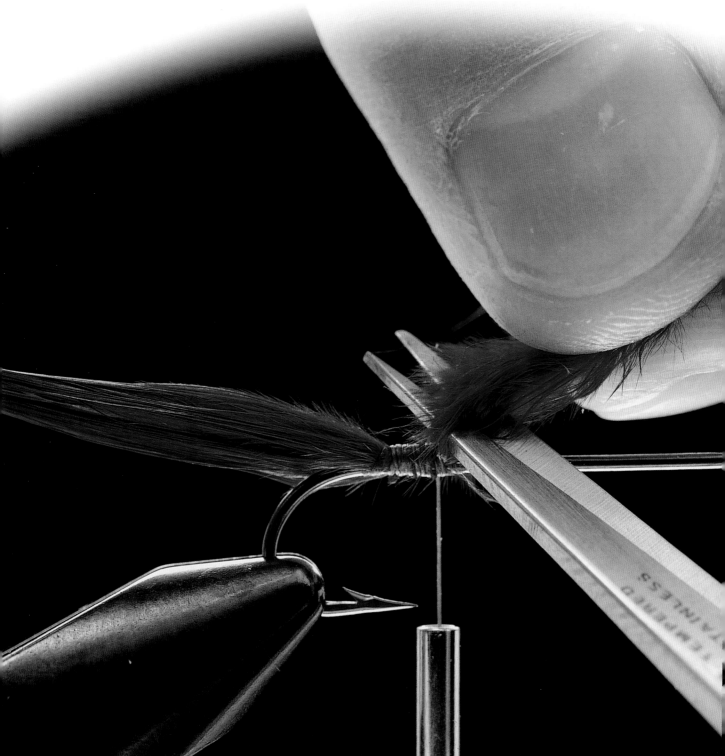

Chapter 5

Making Legs, Adding Eyes & Tying On Tails

159 THREADING RUBBER LEGS

An easy way to thread rubber legs through a cork, balsa, or foam bug body is to file a notch in the eye of a large (darning style) needle, then hook the rubber legs into this open notch, and run the needle with the legs through the body as desired. Once you have the needle and the legs through the body, you can pull on one side of the legs through the hole. If using a double length of leg material for a full leg look, remove the legs from the needle-notched eye and cut the legs at this point with scissors.

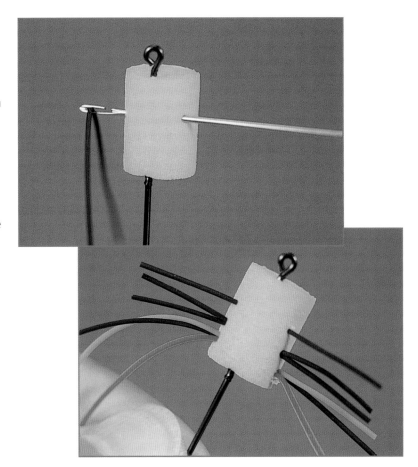

160 MAKING CHENILLE NYMPH LEGS

If you are making large nymphs, such as some Western stonefly nymphs, use fine-diameter Vernille or Ultra Chenille for the legs. These materials are excellent-grade chenilles that you can taper at the ends by heating in a flame and rolling between your fingers. If you want the legs a little stiffer, add some clear flexible sealer to them. Softex is good for this, along with some of the soft epoxies like Soft Head Cement made by Loon Outdoors.

161 RUNNING PILOT HOLES

To run legs through a cork, balsa, or foam body, first make a pilot hole through the side of the bug body with a needle or bodkin. If using a plain needle, first grip the needle in a vise and then run the cork up and down on the needle. Follow this by running a notched-eye needle holding the rubber legs through the cork, foam, or balsa body.

"...impatient sportsmen blame their bad luck."

Sergei Aksakov
Notes on Fishing (1847)
Translated by Thomas
P. Hodge (1997)

162 MAKING HOPPER AND FLY LEGS

Use a small latch-hook tool (they are sold for fly tying in small sizes by fly shops exclusively) to make overhand knots in small bundles of feathers and fibers to make legs for hoppers and other insects.

For best results, do this with the fibers still on the central vane. Make up a bunch of these and you can later clip off what you need when you need it.

163 DRESSMAKER'S PINS FOR EYES

You can make easy eyes for foam, cork, and balsa bugs from plastic-head dressmaker's pins. These come in several sizes and in assorted basic colors including white, black, blue, red, yellow, and green. They are also easy to dress up with an additional dot of paint to make a pupil on each bulging eye.

Cut the stem to a short length with wire cutters (wear safety glasses), and use pliers to insert the eye into the bug body. To keep them in place, add a small dot of glue to the metal stem to glue the stem and the base of the eye in place on the bug.

164 MAKING TANDEM FLIES

One way to make a tandem fly is to tie a few tail materials onto a separate hook and then secure it by means of a mono or wire connector to the main hook. By tying tail materials to the separate tail hook, you essentially extend the length of the fly and also the hooking ability of the fly with this second hook. You can position this hook point up or point down, as preferred.

To do this, add the mono or wire extension to the hook, place it in a vise, and tie on the materials desired. Complete with a whip finish and seal with head cement or epoxy. Place the second hook (forward) in the vise. Then tie the extended wire or mono to the forward hook before adding the materials to complete the fly.

165 BENDING MONOFILAMENT FOR LEGS

To make bent legs from mono for tying some nymphs and realistic imitations, use a flame, soldering iron, or heated cauterizing tool. Hold the mono next to the side of a flame such as you get from a grill starter. (Lighters get too hot to hold.) Do not let the mono touch the flame, since that will melt it. Within a few seconds, the mono will bend from the heat softening the mono at that point.

You can also do this with a hot rod such as a cauterizing tool or electric soldering iron. These tools make a sharper bend in the mono. Make sure that you hold the mono horizontal so that the melted spot causes the extended part of the mono to drop from gravity and make the desired bend.

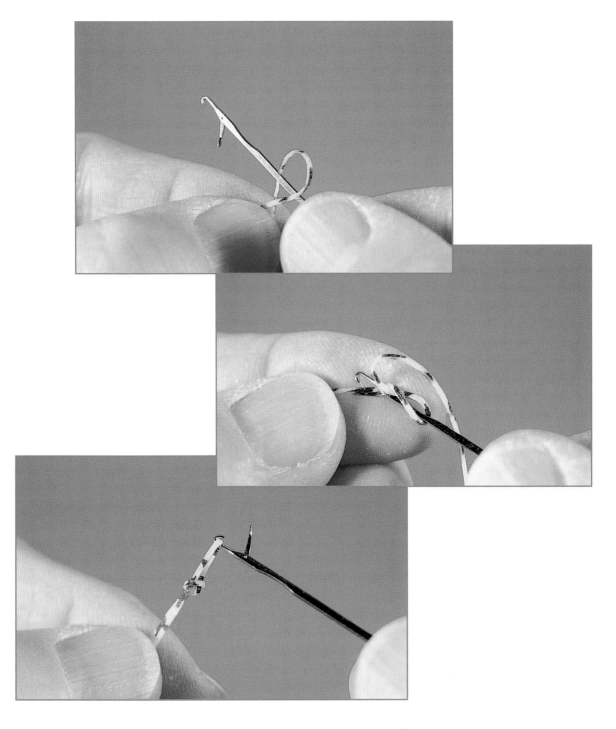

166 MAKING LEGS IN RUBBER MATERIALS

Use the same small-latch tool as on the previous page to make over-hand knots for joints in the rubber legs used for some fly patterns and many bass and panfish bugs. For best results, do this after you have inserted the legs through the bug body. Otherwise, the knot makes pulling the leg through the body difficult. Do this carefully so that the overhand knot makes a neat bent leg right where you want it in the fly.

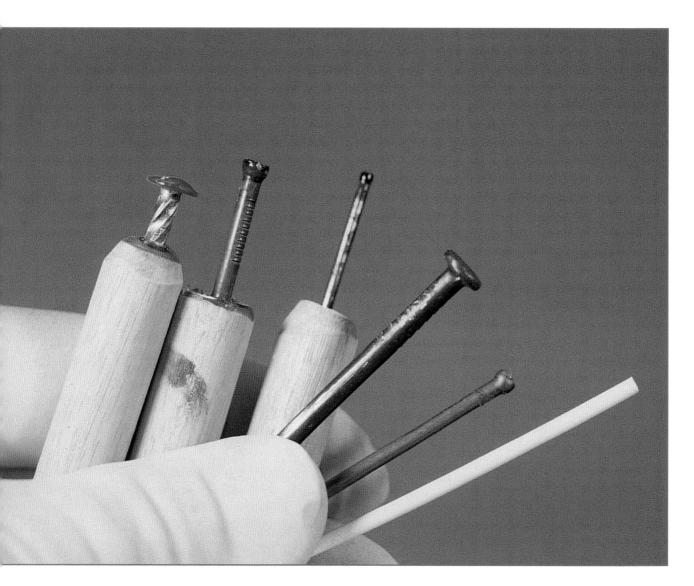

167 MAKING PAINTING STICKS FOR EYES, SPOTS

Make paint sticks to use with liquid paint (small bottles of hobby paint) by sticking a finishing nail or pin into a 4-inch (10.2-cm) length of wood dowel. Make several of these, using different-size pinheads or finishing nails to make different-size eyes and pupils. These are ideal for touching to a puddle of paint to add an eye. Add a pupil by using a smaller pinhead or nail head. Clean the pin or nail with a rag after each use to ready it for the next use.

168 ADDING SELF-STICK EYES PERMANENTLY

Since self-stick eyes seldom stick permanently to the head of any fly, add the self-stick eyes and then protect the eyes with several coatings of fly-head cement or a single coating of epoxy. You most frequently add eyes to large flies, so the epoxy coating is often the best.

MAKING LEGS, ADDING EYES & TYING ON TAILS

169 QUICK AND EASY LEGS

For a quick, easy, and professional way to run rubber legs through a bug body, get a sewing machine needle and cut a notch in the side of the eye with a file or Dremel tool. Then, place needle in a small bench vise with the point up.

To run rubber legs through a foam, cork, or balsa bug, hold the bug sideways over the needle and push down (be careful to keep your fingers out of the way) until the point and notched eye are exposed. Then place the rubber legs in the notch and pull the bug straight up. Do this slowly so that you do not tear or break the rubber legs. Once free of the needle, slip the rubber legs out of the needle notch, and adjust for length. Trim if necessary.

170 ADDING BEAD CHAIN EYES

When adding bead chain, dumbbell, or hourglass eyes to a fly hook, first crisscross the thread over the stem of the eyes that are at right angles to the hook shank. To bind it securely, make several turns of thread horizontally between the hook shank and the eyes. This tightens the previous thread wraps and makes the eyes less likely to twist or rotate around the hook shank. The purpose of all of this is to prevent the eyes from rotating on the hook shank. Add some cyanoacrylate glue to the completed wraps to secure the eyes.

171 MORE EYES

An easy way to make eyes for bugs is with fabric paint. These paints are water-based acrylic, but waterproof once the paint dries for 24 hours. These paints come in opaque and translucent colors, as well as glitter colors. Be sure to get the kind that comes in a bottle or jar with a tapered, pointed nozzle, not those with a flat snap-top lid (like the kind used on ketchup bottles) that makes it harder to dispense. Use the nozzle to dispense just a small dot of paint. If desired, wait until the paint flattens and settles and then add a smaller dot of a contrasting color for a pupil. You can make these in any size for big or small flies.

For best results, create an assembly line where you can lay out a series of bugs, add the eyes to one side, and wait 24 hours as they cure. Turn the bugs over, add eyes to the opposite side, and allow the eyes to cure. You can also use this paint in various colors to paint spots and stripes on bugs, after which you can hang them up to cure. Usually, the fabric paints are viscous enough so that you will not have sags or runs when doing this.

172 TYING SEPARATE BODIES AND TAILS

One way to get extra wiggle in any fly, such as the many large nymph or leech patterns possible, is to tie in a separate tail or body on a separate wire frame, which attaches to the hook with a hinge loop. There are several ways to do this.

One is to tie tail material to a separate ball-eye hook, then cut off (use safety glasses) the hook bend, and attach this tail to a forward fly that you are tying. Do this by first tying down a length of mono, threading the mono through the hook eye of the tail, and then wrapping over the mono loop to make a hinge with the articulated tail.

You can also use any wire for the tail articulated section, using mono loops on both the hook and the tail wire. It is also possible to not remove the hook from the tail so that you have, in essence, a two-hook fly.

Just make sure that any such hook is legal on your waters before using it.

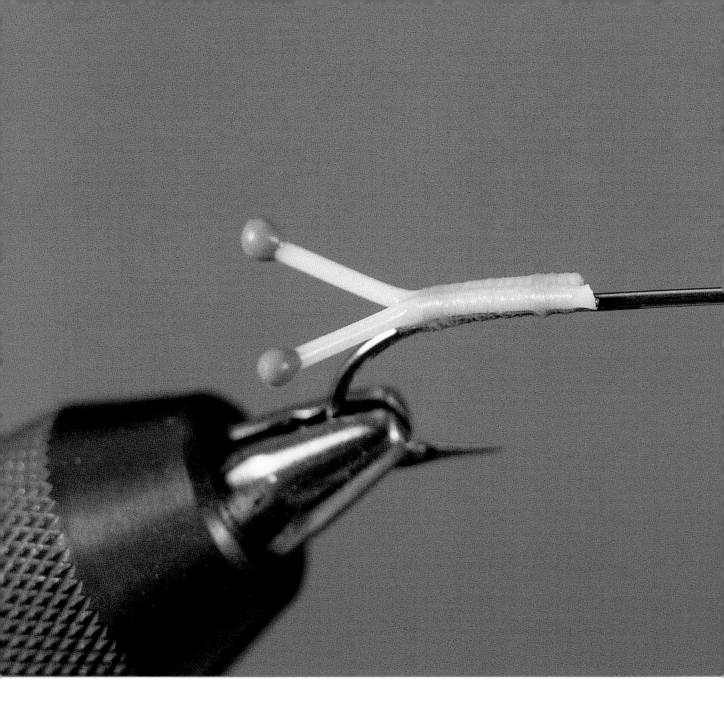

173 MAKING HAIRBRUSH EYES

To make simple eyes for saltwater flies such as shrimp and crabs, use plastic bristles from a hairbrush. These are usually in black, but you can also find other colors. The advantage of these is that they protrude like the eyes of a real shrimp or crab, making the fly more lifelike.

Use wire cutters to cut off two bristles, tie them to the hook shank and bend or flare out the shanks to make the eyes protrude as desired. Bend the plastic bristle at a slight angle or a sharp and right angle, depending upon the position you want for the eyes.

174 MAKING DUMBBELL GLASS/PLASTIC EYES

Make bright plastic or glass bead eyes for flies by placing them on mono. This makes a plastic or glass lightweight equivalent of lead dumbbell eyes or bead chain eyes. You can use any color and size bead for this.

You can get beads in transparent or opaque colors, in red, pink, yellow, green, orange, purple, and other colors. Popular sizes available from tackle supply shops and catalogs include 0.12 inch (3.00 mm), 0.16 inch (4.00 mm), 0.20 inch (5.00 mm), 0.24 inch (6.00 mm), and 0.31 inch (8.00 mm). Beads in other sizes and colors are also available from craft stores.

To do this, first string bright plastic beads onto heavy mono. Use an iron or low-heat soldering iron to melt the end of the mono. Slide two beads against this ball on the end of the mono, grip the mono with needle-nose pliers or tweezers, and cut the mono about 1/16 inch (2 mm) from the pliers. Heat and melt the end of the mono. It is a little more risky, but you can also use an open flame, such as a butane grill lighter.

The result is two beads, with a tying space in the center and the beads held in place with the melted ball on each end of the mono. Repeat as above to make more eyes.

These are ideal as eyes on flies for salmon, steelhead, shad, and similar coastal and anadromous species.

176 SEALING AND PAINTING BULLET-HEAD FLIES

When making bullet heads on flies, such as those in the Thunder Creek series designed by Keith Fulsher (and previously developed as a method of tying by Maine flytier and Gray Ghost originator Carrie Stevens), make sure that you seal the head if you are going to paint eyes on the head. Just as with feather shoulders on flies, you must add some clear sealer to the head so that the painted eye will not bleed when applied to the bunched and folded bucktail head.

177 RECESSING EYES

Eyes on deer-hair bugs always look best if they are recessed. To do this, use a red-hot nail head to burn a recess to hold an eye in the clipped deer-hair body. Once you have burned the recess into the deer hair, add a small amount of glue (Ultra Flex, Ambroid, Duco, etc.) to the recess, and add the chosen eye to the bug.

To make these recess tools, use common nails with the right-size head for the eyes on the flies that you are tying.

Ideal eyes include plastic eyes, movable doll eyes, bright beads.

175 MAKING SPLIT TAILS

Charles Meck, in his book on fly-tying tips, notes an easy way to make split tails on dry flies and nymphs.

To do this, tie in the tail materials and then make a loop of a separate length of tying thread around the bend/shank area of the hook, immediately in back of the tail. Then pull the loop forward, using the joined strands of the loop to split the tail into two or three parts.

To split the tail into two parts, twist the loop strands and bring this between the center of the tail bundle. To make three tails, keep the strands separate and bring them up so that a center part of the tail stays between the loop, and the two split tails angle to the side.

You can adjust the angle of the split tails by the tension on the loop, which pulls forward and is tied down. Then complete the rest of the fly, tying in or wrapping on body materials.

178 ADDING SELF-STICK PRISM EYES

To add self-stick prism eyes to fly heads, use a bodkin to remove the eye from the backing sheet and add it to the head of the fly. Allow the self-stick side of the eye to stick to the bodkin point. Use the bodkin to position the eye on the head of the fly.

179 MAKING FABRIC PAINT EYES ON VINYL

Make painted eyes on vinyl for larger flies. These are tied in place rather than glued to the head. These position the eyes a little farther back on the fly, making a more lifelike appearance.

To do this, buy some clear vinyl from a fabric store. Different thicknesses are available to suit your fly tying and fly size. Then cut this into rectangles about the size of a dollar bill.

From a craft store, get some fabric paint but make sure to buy a brand that has a pointed spout. Get colors for both the eye and pupil color. Make a spot of eye color in two rows on the vinyl patch, followed by a smaller centered dot for the pupil. Good combinations for eye/pupil colors are yellow/black, white/black, orange/black, green/white, blue/white, red/white, red/black.

Once the paints are cured, cut out a pair of eyes by cutting partway around the eye to leave a "tag end" to make a teardrop shape. Tie the eyes by the tag end on each side of the fly so that the eye extends back on the shoulder.

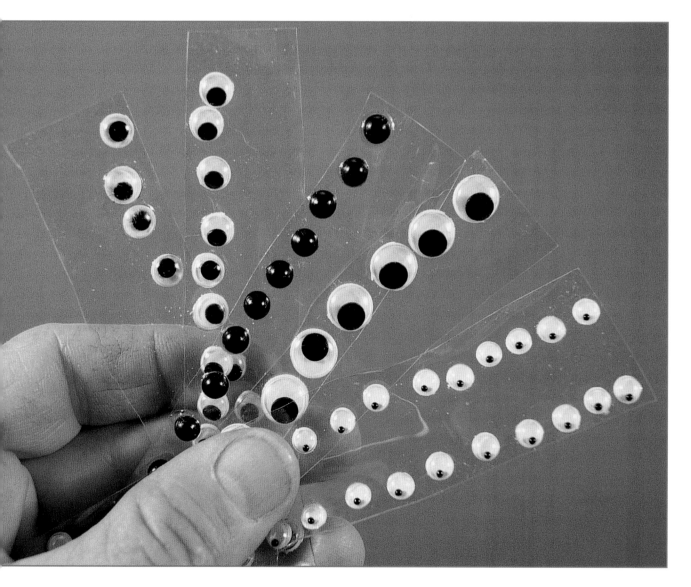

MAKING LEGS, ADDING EYES & TYING ON TAILS

180 MAKING MONO-FILAMENT CRAB AND SHRIMP EYES

One easy way to make eyes for crab and shrimp flies is to use thick monofilament and burn one end to create a ball or "eye." You can make up a number of these in advance and have them ready for your fly tying.

Use 20- to 100-pound-test (9.1- to 45.4-kg) mono for this, depending upon the size of the fly and the size of the ball eye desired. Use a cigarette lighter or fireplace/grill lighter to create them. Color the ball eyes with a black, permanent felt-tip marker.

181 PAINTING DUMB-BELL EYES: ONE

One way to paint lead or non-lead dumbbell or hourglass eyes is to place the eyes between the teeth of a comb for easy holding and paint a number of them at once. This also makes it easy to paint both sides. Allow the paint to cure before removing the eyes from the comb.

182 PAINTING DUMB-BELL EYES: TWO

Another way to paint dumbbell or hourglass eyes is to cut a series of slits, about 1/4-inch (0.6-cm) apart, in a stiff cardboard. Corrugated cardboard is best for this, since it holds the eyes securely and straight out from the cardboard, rather than at an angle where they might fall out as can occur with shirt cardboard. Insert a dumbbell eye into each slit, and paint the eyes as desired.

183 MAKING ANGLED EYES

To make angled eyes for shrimp and other saltwater patterns, wrap 50- to 100-pound (22.7- to 45.4-kg) mono around a square board or square aluminum stock. Use stock that is about 1 to 2 inches (2.5 to 5 cm) square. Secure one end of the mono, then wrap evenly and soak for a few minutes in a pot of boiling water. Remove the wrapped stock from the boiling water and "set" the mono by dipping it in ice water. Once complete, cut the mono down the middle of each stock to make for a lot of mono pieces bent into sharp bends or "elbows." Use a flame to form a ball on one end of this bent mono to make a ball eye. Color the ball with black permanent felt-tip marker. Tie these on the hook shank at the mono elbow to make eyes.

" Fly fishing is to fishing as ballet is to walking."

Howell Raines
Fly Fishing through the Midlife Crisis (1993)

184 TYING RUBBER LEGS

To add rubber legs to a fly or bug (but not through a solid-body bug) center the legs on the hook shank and then criss-cross the tying thread over the rubber legs and hook to hold them in place. The problem with this method is that the pressure on the rubber legs often twists the legs to an odd position on the hook.

A better way is to take the length of rubber leg (or legs), fold it over the tying thread, and then pull the tying thread into the hook shank to position the legs on one side of the fly. Then repeat this on the opposite side of the fly. This is quick and allows more exact placement of the rubber legs.

If you want a bunch of legs in one spot, as when tying a Calcasieu Pig Boat bass fly, you can fold a lot of legs over the thread and pull all into place at once.

185 ADDING DOLL EYES TO FLIES

If using doll eyes that are not self-stick, use a tiny drop of glue to cement the eyes to the head of the fly. Glue both eyes in place, and then lay the fly on a flat area. Do not place the fly on a fly rotator, since this causes the eyes to slightly slide as the glue cures, positioning one eye high on the head and the other eye low.

Once you've glued and cured the eyes, coat the whole head with epoxy. Finally, place the fly on a fly rotator to allow the glue to cure without sagging.

"Perhaps fishing is, for me, only an excuse to be near rivers. If so, I'm glad I thought of it."

Roderick L. Haig-Brown
A River Never Sleeps
(1946)

186 USING A TAPERED-FIBER PAINTBRUSH

Some artist's and household synthetic paintbrushes contain tapered fibers that make excellent, inexpensive tails on dry flies and nymphs. Check hardware, artists supply, and paint stores for these synthetic paintbrushes and buy those that have springy tapered fibers. Most of these are nylon, so you can dye them using Rit or Tintex dyes.

187 ADDING PRISM EYES

To add prism eyes to flies, first crease and fold the eyes in half while they are still on the backing sheet. This is easy to do, since you can fold an entire row of eyes at once. This fold in each eye makes it easier for the eye to conform to the round contour of the fly head.

188 LEGS THAT ANGLE DOWN

If you want rubber legs on a bug to extend at an angle down into the water instead of out at the sides, run a needle with the legs up through the side of the belly and out the center of the back, then from this point in the back down through the bug to exit on the other side of the bug belly.

The result is rubber legs that hang down into the water instead of sticking out from the sides. The effect is different, and also helps to create more action in the bug each time you twitch it.

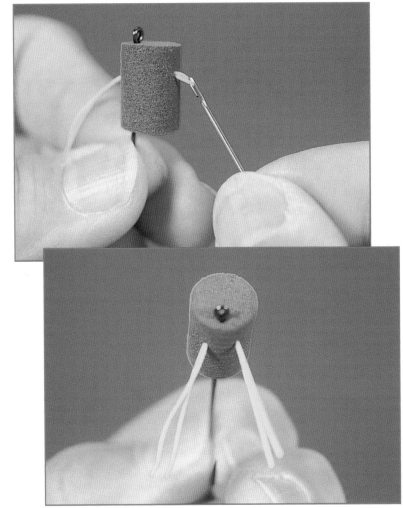

Chapter 6

Tying Bodies, Heads & Ribbing

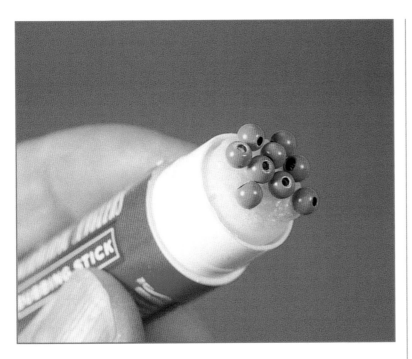

190 BEAD TYING MADE EASY

To control beads when tying bead-head flies, use a stick of dubbing wax and dip it into the bunch of beads, then place the wax stick upright on the bench. The wax tube will hold a number of beads that you can then impale on the hook quickly and easily. If using metal beads, or any beads with a tapered hole, make sure that you insert the hook through the small end of the hole.

189 DETACHED BODIES

There are very thin foam sheeting materials available today, some as thin as 0.02 or 0.04 inches (0.50 or 1.00 mm). The 0.02-inch size is ideal for making detached bodies for flies, typically imitations of mayflies.

For this, cut a long tapered section of foam that you can fold over to make a detached body. To tie these, fold over the thicker end of the foam, attach to the hook shank, and then begin to wrap only around the detached body as you progress toward the tail of the foam. Before you reach it, fold in some tail fibers and wrap over the foam to enclose them. Then reverse the wrap back toward the body of the fly and the hook shank and complete the fly.

The result is a detached body mayfly imitation that floats high as a result of the foam body. These are best to tie when making large imitations.

191 BEAD HANDLING MADE EASY

You can handle beads more easily with a small finger-cot bead holder, available from any craft or sewing store. This fits on the end of a finger and has rough finger-like projections to allow picking up several beads at once. This makes it easy to thread the hook into the bead without having to pick up one bead at a time.

192 AVOIDING LUMPS

When tying on thick materials, such as leather or chamois to make leeches or vinyl to make crayfish or crabs, the thick material can make a lump at the tie-down point. To prevent this, taper the materials to a point and tie this point in before wrapping the material around the hook shank or folding it over the body.

"I chose my cast, a march brown and a dun, and ran down to the river, chasing hope."

Wilfred S. Blunt
A New Pilgrimage (1889)

193 CUTTING VINYL FOR CRAB FLIES

To cut out oblong shapes of cloth-backed vinyl for crab bodies, use a plastic elliptical template, available from art supply and drafting/engineering stores. These templates include many sizes and shapes of various ellipses that simulate the shape of a crab shell.

Pick the size and shape that you need, trace the shape on the vinyl, and then cut out the shapes for use when tying crab flies. Trace the shape on the underside of the vinyl so that you do not mar the top part that is the back of the crab.

194 MAKING A CARAPACE

Use strips of clear vinyl (available in a craft or sewing store) to make the carapace, or back, of shrimp flies and larger flies for saltwater. This is available in several thicknesses in clear, transparent rose, blue, yellow, and green. It is easy to make the back or carapace of shrimp and crab imitations, along with those of sand fleas and mole crabs.

Cut to shape, place on top of a fly body and spiral wrap thread to make a lifelike segmented carapace. Since the underlying materials show through the vinyl, good body materials to use include cactus chenille, chenille, yarn, even dubbing.

195 CLOTH-BACKED VINYL

Cloth-backed vinyl, available from fabric stores, makes great carapace material when tying imitations of crayfish, hellgrammites, large stoneflies, and others. Good colors of vinyl include brown, tan, orange, black, maroon, chocolate, and gray.

You can also make neat saltwater crabs by making a glued "sandwich" of light tan or brown for the carapace and cream for the abdomen.

196 HOT GLUING FLY BODIES

When making flies with large bodies, hot glue is a good option. Doug Brewer first developed and popularized this method of making hot-glue bodies. He uses mini glue guns and colored glue (available through his shop) to make hot-glue-body flies for bonefish, steelhead, panfish, and other species. The basic technique for this is to tie the tail of the fly and then use the hot glue gun to add a round or flattened body to the fly to seal the wraps and the tail in place.

197 USING CERAMICS FOR FLY BODIES

You can use Sculpy and similar products (clay-like materials that are molded and then heated in the oven to cure) to make fly underbodies. You can mold the hard ceramic-like material into any shape, place it on a hook, and then cure it to make the bodies or underbodies for crabs, crayfish, minnows, shrimp, large-head flies, or bonefish-style patterns. The material comes in a lot of different colors, so you can use it as is, paint it, or cover it with other fly-tying materials.

198 ANOTHER WAY TO DUB FLIES

Flytier Chuck Edghill has figured out another way to add dubbing to hooks. To avoid making a loop in the tying thread for adding dubbing when making a dubbed body, you can use the tag end of the working thread left from tying on, along with the working thread.

To do this, leave a long tag end when you first tie the thread to the hook and position this tag end at the end or bend of the hook if not tying down there. Then work on the rest of the fly up to the point of adding the dubbing at the rear. For this, wrap the working thread back to the rear of the hook shank, and then wax this working thread and the tag end of thread.

Add the dubbing between the two threads and then grip the two threads with hackle pliers. Twist or spin to capture the dubbing material. Wrap the dubbing with the two threads around the body, strip the excess dubbing from the thread when complete, tie down the tag end thread, and then clip all excess. Do not clip the working thread, which is necessary to complete the fly.

199 TINSEL

For a thicker but smooth tinsel body, wind tinsel over a thread base. To do this, tie in the thread at the head of the fly, immediately in back of the hook eye. Then tie in the tinsel and wrap the thread evenly around the hook shank and the tinsel all the way back to the bend of the hook. Reverse the thread wrap and make a smooth wrap all the way up to the head of the fly. Then wrap the tinsel around the rear of the hook shank, bring it up onto the smooth thread base, and wrap evenly to the head of the fly. Tie off the tinsel with the working thread and continue with the remainder of the fly.

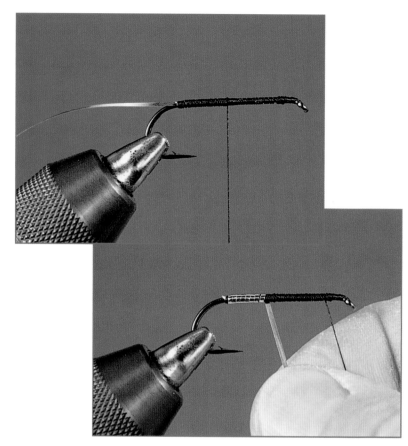

200 GETTING TIGHT WRAPS WITH TINSEL

When adding metallic tinsel, make each wrap so that it starts to slightly overlap the previous wrap. Then pull down so that the tinsel slides off of the previous wrap and falls into perfect position.

You can both hear and feel this "snap" of tinsel as it seats into place on the hook shank as you make each turn. This ensures that each wrap of the tinsel is tight against the previous wrap to make a smooth, shiny tinsel body.

201 METAL TINSEL

While Mylar tinsel and other plastic wraps are gaining more and more favor with flytiers, there is a place for the old-time metallic tinsel. This is tougher and a fish is less likely to cut through it than the Mylar or plastic wraps. If tying flies exclusively for toothy fish, or if your flies might be used for toothy critters, make sure that you use the tougher metallic tinsel in place of Mylar or plastic.

202 DOUBLE WRAP TINSEL

To make an easy tinsel body, double wrap it after tying on at the head of the fly. For this, tie the working thread down in back of the hook eye and then tie down a length of tinsel. Wrap the tinsel down the hook shank to the bend and then reverse it to wrap the tinsel back up the hook shank. Tie off at the head. Then you can tie on a wing, shoulders, and other fly parts to make a simple streamer.

You can only do this if you do not include a tail in the fly. If you do include a tail or oval tinsel ribbing, you will have to wrap over these materials with thread after tying them down.

"Calling fishing a hobby is like calling brain surgery a job."

Paul Schullery
Mountain Time (1984)

203 MAKING STREAMLINED TINSEL BODIES

To keep from making a lump when adding metallic tinsel, cut the tinsel at a sharp angle, and tie this angled end down in place. This makes for smooth winding of the tinsel without a lump at the tie-down point. This is particularly important on small and delicate dry flies.

204 TWISTING DUBBING

Make sure that you only twist one way when adding dubbing to waxed thread or a dubbing loop. If you twist both directions when adding dubbing, it will not stay on the fly. The single direction twist also ensures that the dubbing looks lifelike.

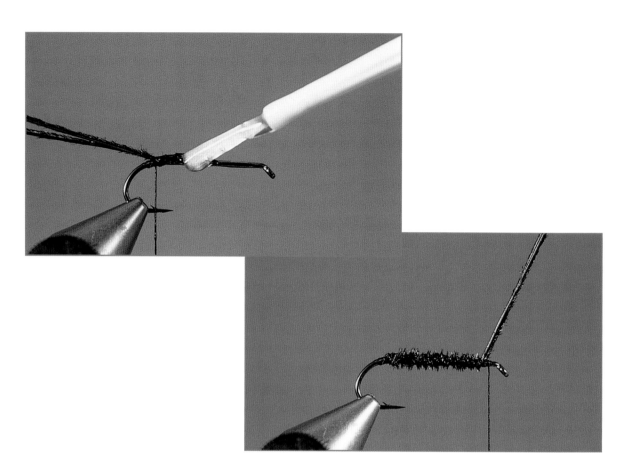

206 PEACOCK HERL

Peacock herl is fragile, but one way to make a peacock-herl-bodied fly more durable is to coat the hook shank or under-body with glue right before wrapping the peacock herl in place. This glues the peacock herl to the hook shank, without affecting the look or iridescence of the fly. The glue may not pre-vent a toothy fish from cutting the herl, but it prevents the herl from unraveling, preserving the look of the fly.

205 TWISTING PEACOCK HERL WITH THREAD

To reinforce fragile materials, such as peacock herl, wrap and twist the peacock herl and the working thread together, and then wrap this combined strand of thread and peacock herl around the hook shank to form the body.

Once at the tie-off point, separate the peacock herl and the thread, tie off the peacock herl with the thread, and then clip off the excess.

207 SOFTENING QUILLS

To keep the quill bodies of your dry flies from breaking and cracking, soak them in warm water first. This softens the quill body so that you can wrap it around the hook shank without risking the quill breaking.

If you are going to use a number of quills for a lot of tying, you can soak them together and then place them in a zipper-sealed plastic sandwich bag. That way you can remove a few at a time to use while the remainder stay moist.

210 COUNTER-WRAPPING RIBS

To prevent fragile body materials from becoming frayed and undone when fished, add a rib. But instead of wrapping the rib in the same direction as the body material, counter-wrap it by going around the hook shank in the opposite direction of that used for wrapping the body. Fine wire is especially good as a reinforcement rib for fragile bodies.

208 PROTECTING OVERBODIES

If tying with lead or non-lead wire on the hook shank to weight the fly, the wire may discolor any overwrap of floss or yarn. To prevent this, wrap over the wire with the tying thread and seal with head cement or nail polish to protect overlying body materials. For a quicker step in doing this, avoid the tying thread wrap and coat the wire with head cement before continuing. Allow the cement to cure before adding any overwrap body materials.

209 MAKING RIBBING

To make an easy body ribbing on any fly, leave a long tag end of the tying thread when tying on. Allow for a tag end about 8 inches (20.3 cm) long. Do not cut it. Then tie in the tail and body, and wind the thread forward. Wind the body forward and tie off with the thread. Then use the tag end of thread to spiral around the body to create a ribbed effect.

This looks best if the body and thread (ribbing) are of contrasting colors.

211 TWISTING PEACOCK HERL

Another way to reinforce peacock herl is to tie in several or more strands of the material for a body, then wind the thread forward. To strengthen the peacock herl, twist the strands together and then wrap the twisted strands around the hook shank to form the body. You can make this twist of peacock herl a tight wrap or a loose wrap, depending on the type of look that you want in the finished fly. The loose wrap will appear a little shaggier, while a very tight wrap will appear neater and more compact. It is also tougher and harder for a fish to tear up.

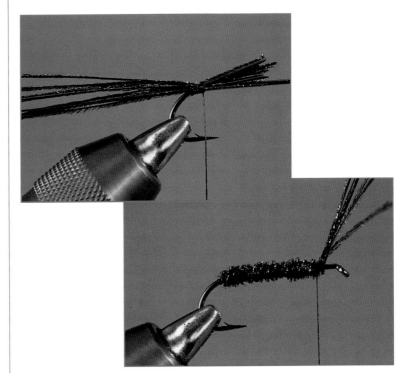

212 PROTECTING QUILL BODIES: ONE

Quill bodies from peacock herl, such as those used to tie quill-body flies, are very fragile. Tie the fly. Then, when you have several or more identical flies tied, coat the quill bodies with head cement to seal and protect the wrapped quill.

213 PROTECTING QUILL BODIES: TWO

Another way to protect quill bodies on flies is to first coat the hook shank or underbody with a head cement or thin glue. Then wrap the stripped quill in place over the wet glue to cement it in place before tying off at the head of the fly.

214 PROTECTING QUILL BODIES: THREE

A third way to protect a quill body is to first tie down a length of fine mono—about 8X tippet or 1- or 2-pound-test (0.5- or 0.9-kg)—to the rear of the hook shank at the same time that you tie down the stripped quill. Then wind the thread forward, followed by the wrap of stripped quill, which you then tie off.

At this point, counterwrap (spiral wrap in the opposite direction) the mono to protect the quill body from breaking and tie off the mono at the head of the fly. The quill shows through the fine mono used for this.

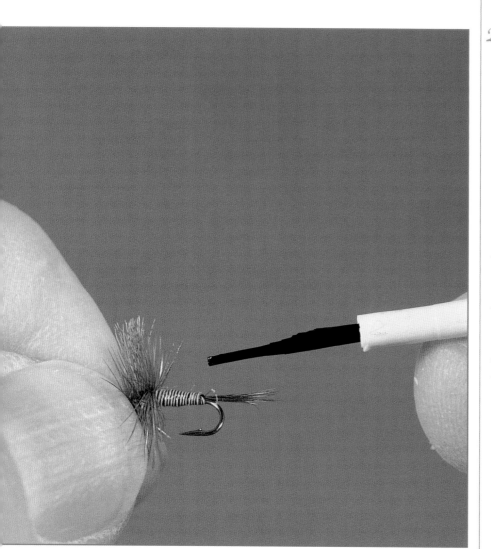

TYING BODIES, HEADS & RIBBING

215 TWISTING YARN

To get a more ribbed or segmented look in a small fly, tightly twist two or more strands of very fine yarn and wrap this around the hook shank for a body.

The two different colors of yarn make a ribbed look, without the necessity of tying the body and then tying a separate ribbing over the body. You can also vary this by how tight you twist the two colors of yarn.

216 THREAD-BODIED MIDGES

To tie a tiny fly, tie a thread-bodied midge. Pick a tying thread the color of the midge body you want, tie on, and then wrap evenly to the rear and then back to the front of the fly. Finish with a wrap or two of peacock herl or dubbing material of your choice.

Another way is to first add a bead to the fly hook (glass, plastic, or metal) and then tie the thread body.

217 REMOVING FUZZ FROM PEACOCK

Use an eraser to remove the fuzz from peacock herl to make quill bodies for flies such as the Quill Gordon. Try an "ink" eraser, which is a little harder and usually works better than a pencil eraser.

Lay the peacock herl fiber out on a flat surface, hold one end, and use the eraser to rub in one direction only (away from the end you are holding). Do this gently so as to not break the fiber.

218 LARGE PEACOCK QUILL BODIES

To make large bodies of peacock quills, use two or more to completely cover the hook shank. For best results, tie in both together and then wrap the two together around the hook shank. Since you are using two fibers, you cover more hook shank with each wrap, thus covering the hook shank rapidly.

"You can't say enough about fishing. Though the sport of kings, it's just what the deadbeat ordered."

Thomas McGuane
In Silent Seasons, Edited by Russell Chatham
(1978)

219 MAKING MINNOW BODIES

You can use a lot of different materials to make "skeletons" for minnow shapes covered by braided Mylar or other tubing materials designed to make minnow bodies. Some possibilities for this include flat, stiff, foam materials such as is used for packaging and sheet plastic. You can use stiff, thick cardboard if you cover it with a sealer such as waterproof glue, epoxy, or a few layers of head cement.

Cut the material into the desired minnow shape and length, position it on the hook, and spiral wrap and crisscross with the tying thread to secure it until you can cover it with the tubing material. Often this is best wrapped and secured to the top of the hook shank so that you do not reduce the gap of the hook. If you wrap it underneath the hook shank, make sure you taper it in the back to provide good hook gap.

After securing and sealing the body shape, cover the skeleton with a length of tubing tied in place at both ends. Long-shank hooks are best for these minnow imitations.

220 TYING EMERGERS AND SHUCKS

Of recent interest in fly tying is the tying of emerger insect imitations, which have a trailing shuck (the leftover skin or casing from their days underwater as a nymph, and from which they have emerged as an adult winged insect). One good way to make this and still keep the fly afloat in the surface film is to tie in a tiny piece of foam at the rear of the hook shank, then veil it with a few light-colored, soft hackle fibers. This makes it appear broken and discarded as with a real shuck. Then tie the rest of the fly as normal, concentrating on a surface floating or comparadun style that floats in the surface film.

Good foam material includes the tiny beads of foam that are part of polyfoam packaging material. These "beads" of foam are easily broken or rubbed off of blocks of packaging material foam.

221 HACKLE CONTROL: ONE

Use a short length of a plastic straw to push back the hackle of a wet or dry fly to make it easier to finish the head and make a whip finish. You can also use a small strip or sheet of plastic, formed into a funnel shape by folding it around itself. Because of the angled shape, this is usually best for wet fly hackle.

To do this without slitting the material for the thread, slip the material onto the bobbin before tying down. Then slide the straw or material into place when tying off.

222 HACKLE CONTROL: TWO

Another way to hold back hackle of wet flies or dry flies when finishing the head or tying a whip finish, is to cut a slit in a small piece of paper, and then slide this over the eye and head to hold the hackle back. The slit in the paper is necessary to pull the thread forward to tie off the fly.

Then form the paper into a slight cone by overlapping the cut edges of the paper and pulling back the hackle. Wrap with the thread to secure and position the hackle in a tapered position. Form the head with the thread, tie off with a whip finish, and cut the thread to complete.

223 MAKING FUZZY BODIES

To make a fuzzy body that has the undulating and moving lifelike appearance of a nymph insect, use the blood feather from marabou. The blood feather on any bird is the feather that grows from the base of each feather stem and is very fluffy and webby. By tying this down and wrapping around the body, it is easy to create a soft, buggy-looking fly.

To make this a little less buggy and to protect the marabou blood feathers, leave a long tag end of thread, and after wrapping the marabou forward, follow by a wrap or counterwrap of the thread, spiral wrapped around the marabou blood feather body.

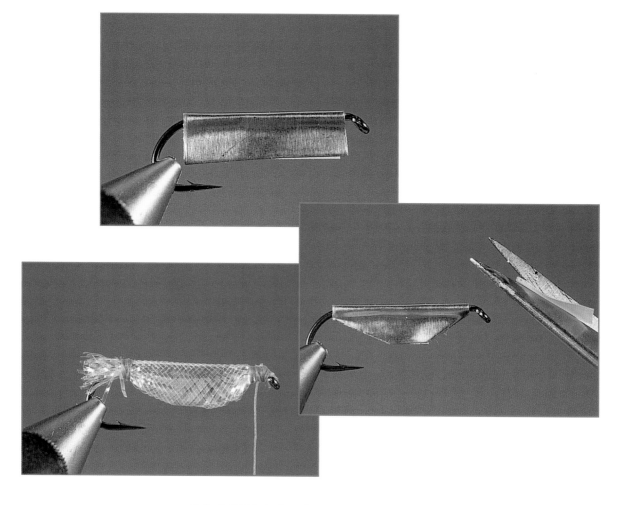

224 SHAD OR SMELT BODIES

Flies that imitate smelt, menhaden, sunfish, or shad must have deep bodies that closely resemble these baitfish. One way to do this (and to weight the fly at the same time) is to use lead or non-lead tape cut into a small rectangle. Most of this tape is self-stick. Center the metal tape on top of the hook shank, then fold the tape over the hook shank so that the two parts of the tape touch (stick together). Cut the front and rear of the tape at an angle so that the body resembles a deep shad shape. Cover this body base with Mylar or similar tubing, tied off at the front and rear to make a shiny fish body.

225 SMOOTH AND TAPERED BODIES

Bodies on flies should be neat and smooth, or at least not lumpy at the rear. This is especially important when tying a fly designed to imitate a natural insect, such as a mayfly, stonefly, or caddis fly in either adult or nymph form. Sometimes, this can be a problem if tying on tail and body material at this same point. The thread wrap, lump of body material tied down, and tail material can increase the body diameter at the rear. To prevent this, make the tail material the full length of the hook shank. When tying down the body material, leave enough tag end of body material that you can wrap over both the forward part of the tail material and the tag end of the body material when wrapping the thread forward. This makes a smooth body and minimal thread wraps at the end of the hook shank where these two materials combine.

226 BEADS FOR TRAILING SHUCKS

Another way to create a trailing shuck in a surface fly is to slide some beads onto a length of monofilament, seal off one end with a lighter to create a ball, and tie in the mono on the hook shank with the beads trailing in back.

Use pearl or similar iridescent beads. Then veil these with some hackle fibers to disguise the beads and make them more lifelike as a trailing shuck.

227 TRANSLUCENT LOOK

To get a translucent look to a fly body, wrap the hook shank with a base-color thread or tinsel and then overwrap with a thin layer of floss, yarn, or dubbing. Experiment by placing your flies in water to see which material combination works well for this look. A good combination is Gudebrod EZ-Dub over a solid thread body. White EZ-Dub is designed so that it becomes translucent when wet to allow underlying materials to show through.

228 NON-WEIGHTED SMELT BODIES

An easy way to make a non-weighted body for a smelt pattern is to use one that Maine tyer Charlie Mann developed. To do this, cut a length of a tapered Stim-U-Dent toothpick, cut and taper the blunt end, and then glue it under the hook shank and wrap with thread. Cover this with a wrap of tinsel or shiny braid tubing or slide a length of Mylar tubing over the body base. Tie off the tubing at both ends to make a body, and finish the fly.

229 ISOLATING DRY-FLY WINGS

To isolate wings when tying divided wing or spent wing mayflies, wind a few turns of thread around the base of each wing after separating the wing with crisscross and figure-eight wraps. The individual turns of thread around each wing help to support it, hold it erect, divide it, and maintain the upright, divided wing.

230 FOLDING HACKLE

To make some flies, you need to fold the hackle, using the stem as a fold point. Such tying methods are ideal for salmon flies, some wet flies, flies palmered with hackle, and soft hackle spey-type flies. You can do this easily without one of the costly tools made for this purpose. One way is to use an old, discarded book.

Place the book in a rack with the open side (pages) up, with the pages slightly loose. Then hold the hackle by the stem at both ends (use two hands), lightly insert the hackle, and "saw" the hackle stem into and between the open pages. The result is that the pages naturally fold the hackle fibers over. Press the pages together, leave the hackle there for a while, and then remove as desired for tying onto the hook.

You can also prepare a number of hackles this way by preparing and folding the hackles between different pages of the book. This keeps each hackle separate, but folded and stored in this position.

231 CHECKING AND IDENTIFYING FLY HACKLE

You can identify dry fly and wet fly hackle by the webbing. Wet fly hackle has a wide, large webbing area that extends up the central vane of the feather. Dry fly hackle has little or very thin webbing. The result is that dry fly hackle absorbs little moisture, making it ideal to float a fly on the surface, while webby wet fly hackle absorbs water and sinks.

232 SPEY FLIES

Sparse is good when tying spey and other soft hackle flies. With these longer soft hackles, you get more action and seemingly more movement and lifelike wiggles out of a sparsely dressed or palmered hackle spey/soft hackle fly.

Do this by making only one or two turns of the hackle around the hook shank before tying it off. Also be sure to use hen hackle or the soft butt fibers of a hackle stem that gives you the action desired.

233 HEN HACKLE FOR SOFT-HACKLE WET FLIES

Use hen hackle when making soft-hackle wet flies. Hen hackle is easier to get than some of the exotics such as partridge or grouse feathers, and makes for a softer, more "alive" hackle than the stiffer rooster hackles used for most dry flies.

In using this material for soft or spey hackle flies, realize that the hackle should be longer than that used in standard wet flies. For most wet flies, hackle (or throat hackle) should be only long enough to hit the point of the hook. For soft-hackle flies, the hackle is often up to twice as long as the hook shank for added movement and action in the water.

234 HEAD CEMENT SUBSTITUTE

If short of head cement for finishing and sealing the thread wraps and head of your flies, you can use clear fingernail polish. A favorite of many flytiers is Sally Hansen Hard As Nails. You can also use colored nail polish to give a different look to the fly and to make colored heads on flies.

Chapter 7

Working With Cork, Foam & Balsa

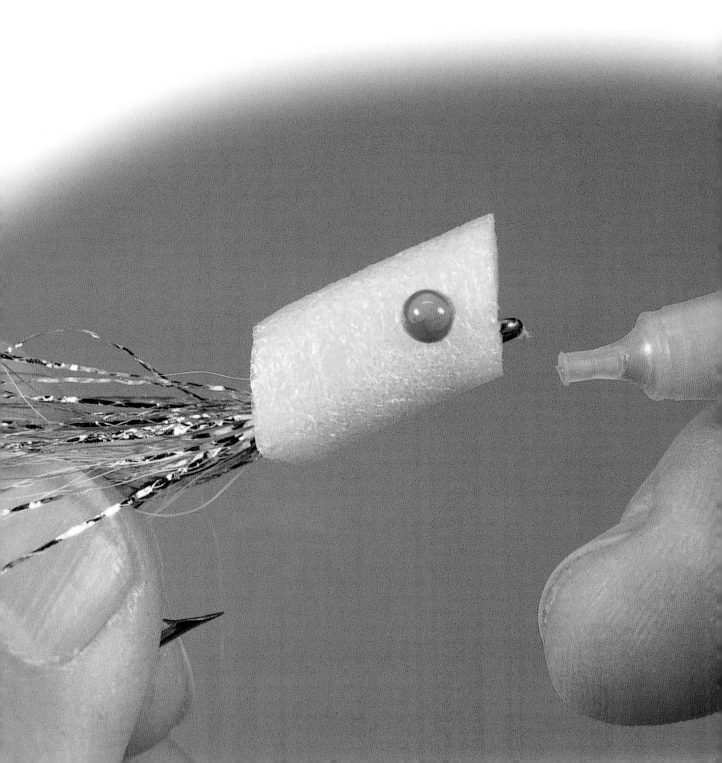

235 SHAPING FOAM BODIES

One way to shape foam bodies is to use a flame (lighter or grill-starter) to slightly heat the foam, and then roll it with your fingers (be careful to not burn yourself) to form the foam into a tapered or rounded shape. This works best with lightweight foam bodies or pre-cut foams used to make beetles, ants, jassids, hoppers, crickets, termites, and other terrestrial fly patterns. This tapering and rounding makes a more natural body appearance in any fly.

236 HIDING TAIL WRAPS

To hide the wrap of tail material on a foam bug body, use a triangle tapered cutter in a Dremel-type tool to make a tapered opening in the rear of the bug. Tie the tail, flash, collar, etc., on the hook so that the bug body buries these wraps.

Soak the hook and the tail thread wrap with CA glue and force the hook into the pilot hole in the bug until seated properly. Done properly, the foam body completely hides the wrap used to hold the tail.

"Quite possibly this is the key to fishing: the ability to see glamour in whatever species one may fish for."

Harold Blaisdell

The Philosophical Fisherman (1969)

237 GLUING HOOKS IN BUG BODIES

When tying bass bugs, the simplest way to make a tight glue bond of the hook into the cork or balsa body is to wrap the hook shank with heavy, coarse thread. Use size "D," "E," or "EE" thread (used for rod wrapping). Spiral wrap the thread up and down the hook shank and tie off with a whip finish. This is important even when using kink- or hump-shank hooks designed for bass bugs.

"No sport affords a greater field for observation and study than fly fishing, and it is the close attention paid to the minor happenings upon the stream that marks the finished angler."

George M. L. La Branche
The Dry Fly and Fast Water (1914)

238 THE STRONGEST BONDS FOR BUG BODIES

For the strongest bond of a hook in a cork or balsa body, first tie on regular fly-tying thread and then tie on and wrap the hook with chenille or yarn. Tie off with the thread.

Make a large slot in the cork or balsa body, and then soak the chenille/yarn-wrapped hook with five-minute epoxy, add some epoxy in the wide slot, and insert the hook. Add a little more epoxy on top of this and remove any epoxy that seeps from the two ends.

Tests have shown that this is the strongest of all possible methods of gluing a hook into a cork or balsa body, even though it takes a little more time to complete. This works well for both plain- and hump-shank hooks.

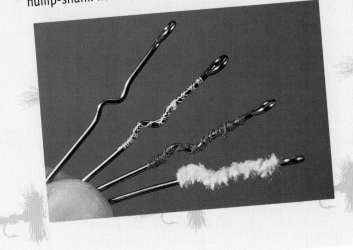

239 SLOTTING BUG BODIES FOR THE HOOK

To make a slot to hold a hook in a cork- or balsa-body bass popper or slider, use a fine-tooth hacksaw blade. Unlike using a razor blade, which only creates a cut, a hacksaw blade slot leaves room for the thread-wrapped hook and for the glue bond.

240 SLOTTING BUG BODIES FOR CHENILLE-WRAPPED HOOKS

To make a slot for a chenille-wrapped hook when gluing a hook into a cork or balsa body, use three to four hacksaw blades wrapped together. For best results, use fine-tooth blades (32 teeth per inch/2.5 cm) and alternate the tooth direction of adjoining blades for quick and easy cutting.

241 AEROSOL PAINTING OF BASS BUGS

The best way to get a good, smooth coat of paint on cork or balsa bass bugs is to spray them using an aerosol spray can or a professional-style airbrush. However, this often sprays paint on the hook as well. To prevent this, you can "mask" the hook and hook shank area with a fold of cardboard that fits around the hook shank as you hold it.

If you wish to paint bug bodies in an assembly line, you can use a long strip of corrugated cardboard and slip a number of hook shanks into the corrugated cardboard where you can spray them all at once. You can also spray them from both sides with the hook point and shank completely protected.

Another option is to make up a slotted corkboard to hold the hook shanks for repeated assembly-line operations.

242 PAINTING FRAMES

An ideal frame for holding the tulle or scale netting for spraying scales on bugs is one of the spray frames used to hold needlepoint work. These are available from craft and sewing stores in a number of sizes and shapes.

243 PAINTING BUGS

If gluing or painting cork, foam, or other materials to a hook shank to which you have already added rubber legs, do not let the paint or glue touch the legs. Often synthetic legs curl and bend from contact with liquid paint or glue, making them unnatural or unusable afterward.

244 HOLDING SPRAY-PAINTED BUG BODIES

When spray painting cork- or balsa-body bugs, use an inexpensive pair of needle-nose pliers to hold the hook. Best are long needle-nose pliers to hold the bug by the hook and allow spray painting without the risk of painting your hand. You can also use wide-jaw pliers to hold bugs by the hook, since the wider jaws help to mask the hook and protect it from paint.

245 GLOVES FOR PAINTING BUG BODIES

An alternative way to spray paint cork- and balsa-body bugs is to buy inexpensive latex gloves from a discount or drug store. These are disposable and available in packs of ten or a hundred. Hold the hook while spraying to prevent getting paint on your skin and discard the gloves after each painting session.

246 PAINTING STEPS FOR BUGS

When painting cork- or balsa-body bass bugs, it is always best to use a coat of primer and then two coats of white paint. This is absolutely necessary if painting a top or final coat that is pale, pastel, or fluorescent. Without the undercoat of white, lighter colors will appear muddy, dull, and unnatural.

247 SCALE FINISH ON BUGS

Want scales painted onto your cork or balsa bug body? This is easy. Get some scale netting from a fly or tackle shop or buy tulle (a type of netting material) from a craft or fabric store.

First paint a base coat of the scale color desired. Then stretch and hold the netting over the bug, and spray a second time with a contrasting color of paint. The result is a scale finish.

If you want light scales, use a light or white base coat and then spray through the netting with a dark color. For dark scales, use a dark undercoat and spray through the netting with a light or white aerosol paint.

Since most bugs and lures are spray painted with scale finishes only on the sides (not the top or belly), the best way to do this is to mount the scale netting in a frame and hold it tight against the bug body when spraying.

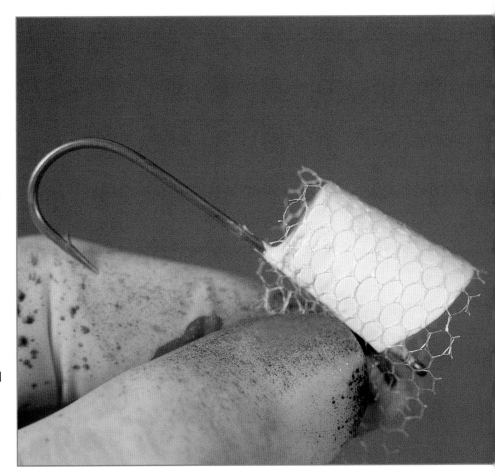

248 MAKING SEGMENTED BODIES

You can make segmented tails of large insects, such as dragonflies, using a neat trick I first learned from creative flytier Bill Skilton. By this method, you can make segmented extended bodies or tails formed by wraps of thread around lengths of foam. This is not just spiral wrapping the thread around the body as is done on bodies formed on a hook shank.

To do this, prepare a long, thin strip of foam twice the length of the desired tail. Tie the working thread in the middle. Then fold the foam strip in half at the point where you tied in the tying thread. To make this step and following steps easy, fold the foam over a long needle placed in your fly-tying vise, with the fold/tied part next to the vise jaws. Then run the thread between the two foam strips, followed by making two wraps around both foam strips and the central hidden needle. Do this where you want the first segment.

Following this, again run the thread between the two foam strips and repeat the above at the junction of the next two segments. When you achieve the desired segmented length, pull the extended body from the needle. Remove the needle from the vise and add a

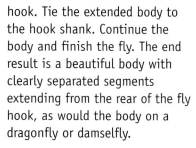

hook. Tie the extended body to the hook shank. Continue the body and finish the fly. The end result is a beautiful body with clearly separated segments extending from the rear of the fly hook, as would the body on a dragonfly or damselfly.

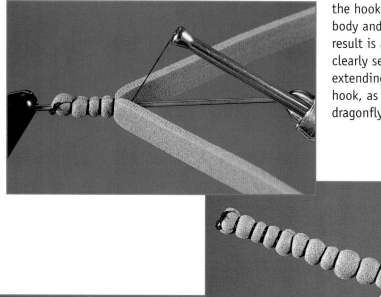

WORKING WITH CORK, FOAM & BALSA

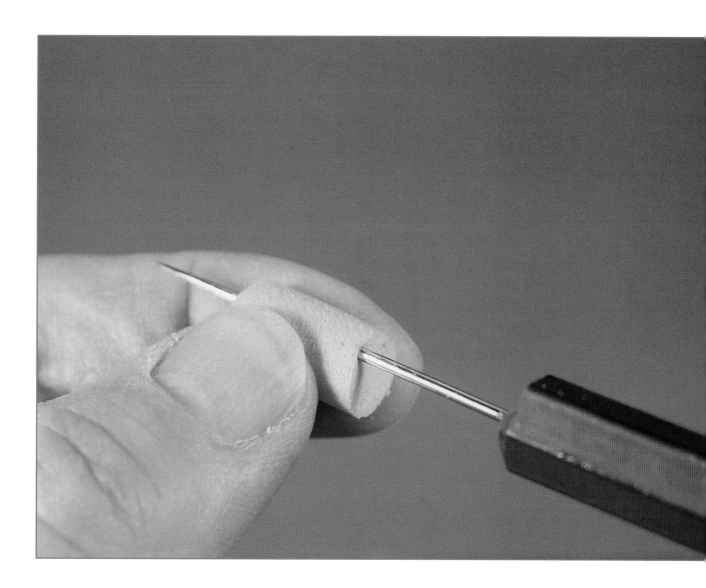

249 MAKING HOLES FOR GLUING HOOKS

You do not need to make a slot to hold a hook in a closed-cell foam bug body. To secure the hook, use a bodkin to make a hole through the belly of the bug body to serve as a pilot hole for the hook shank. Make the hole as close to the skin as possible to preserve the hook gap of the fly.

"If a new man is particularly attentive he can learn to fly fish in a half hour. But then he will go on learning as long as he fishes for trout."

Arthur R. Macdougall, Jr.
"Rods and Rods"
The Trout Fisherman's Bedside Book (1963)

250 GLUING INTO FOAM

To glue a hook shank into a foam bug body, spiral wrap the hook shank with thread and tie off. Coat the hook shank with CA glue (cyanoacrylate cement) and force the hook, eye first, through the pilot hole previously formed and into the rear of the bug. Align the hook with the bug body before the glue sets up.

251 ADDING COLOR TO FOAM TERRESTRIALS

When tying foam terrestrials for trout or panfish, consider adding a final wrap to secure a small square of bright red, orange, or yellow foam on top. This allows you to track the fly better in rough water or where there is a lot of detritus on the surface. The square of color does not affect your fishing, since the fish only see the underside or side of the fly, not the top.

252 EYE-BUSTING PAINT IN HOOK EYES

To get the paint out of the eye of a painted bug body, use an "eye-buster" tool, designed to remove the paint from jig heads. These are available from most tackle shops.

For best results, do this shortly after the paint has cured, since it becomes harder and more difficult to remove with time. Also, the harder and older paint gets, the more likely it is to chip or flake.

253 LEAVING CLEARANCE FOR PAINT ON BUGS

If you add several coats of paint or enamel to your cork or balsa popping bugs, leave about 1/16 inch (2 mm) of bare shank in back of the eye as clearance for the paint buildup. If you seat and glue the popping cork to the hook with the head touching or right in back of the hook eye, subsequent coats of paint will clog the eye making it impossible to clean without damaging the paint on the bug face. This 1/16-inch clearance allows for paint build-up on the face of the bug without clogging the hook eye.

254 CHOOSING THE RIGHT DIAMETER BUG BODY

If making cork, balsa, or foam poppers or sliders, choose bodies that have a diameter approximately equal to the gap of the hook used. This creates the best proportion and balance on the finished bug. In some cases, you might even want to make bugs that have a body smaller than the gap of the hook, such as making bugs specifically for panfish and bluegills. These fish have very small mouths, so the smallest possible body that will still wake or pop, yet tied on a hook that hooks the fish, makes it easier to unhook the fish.

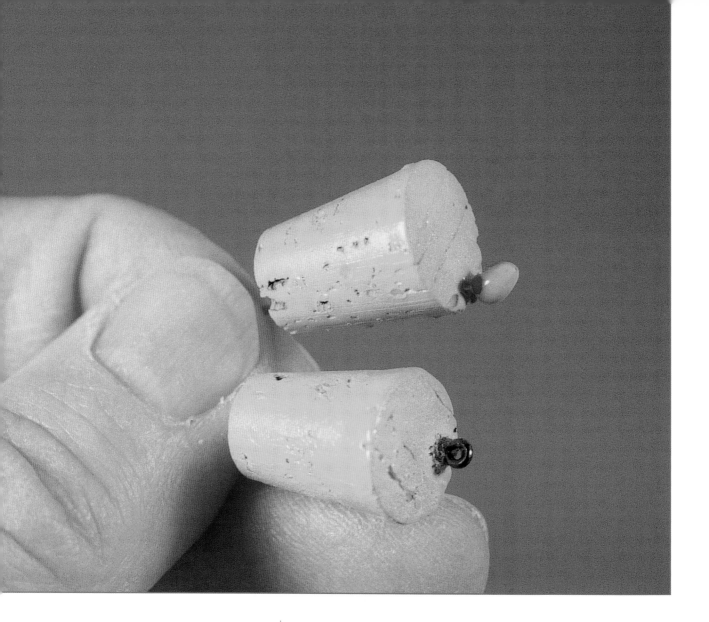

255 WAXING HOOK EYES

If you don't like the idea of scraping or punching out paint from the eye of painted cork and balsa bugs, there is another way to solve this vexing problem. It adds another step, but many flytiers like the convenience it affords.

For this, coat the hook eye of the bug hook with wax before painting. To do this, first complete the bug body by gluing, sealing, and preparing the body for painting. Then dip the hook eye only into molten candle wax to coat the eye. Make sure that you cover only the hook eye, since you do not want wax on the cork or balsa body.

Next, paint the bug body by dipping, spraying or brushing. The wax on the hook eye prevents any paint from adhering. You can easily scrape off any leftover paint with a fingernail. Then finish the bug by tying on the tail, collar, adding rubber legs, etc.

Another way to accomplish this is to use petroleum jelly on the eye of the hook. Test both systems first to make sure that they work with the paint formula that you are using, since different paints have different reactions with various products.

256 CRUDE CORKS CATCH FISH

If you are tying cork bass bugs for your own use and only care about catching fish, you do not have to fill in the pits before painting them. You should still paint with primer, undercoat, and final coats, but the pits won't bother the fish or keep them from hitting. Some very excellent fly anglers do not even paint their bugs, but only fish natural cork bodies glued on a hook and tied with simple tails.

258 FOAM COLOR

When tying foam terrestrials, the color of the foam may not matter much. A trout or panfish looking at a bug from underneath almost always sees the bug in silhouette. Up close, they can distinguish colors if they take time to closely examine a bug. It is best to keep foam bugs to basic colors—black, white, yellow, brown, and green are popular.

257 "SANDWICH" FLIES AND BUGS

You can make bugs by forming a "sandwich" of flat foam materials. These foam sheets are available from fly-tying shops as well as craft stores. If making sandwich bugs, glue the parts of the foam sheeting together using contact cement or a spray adhesive, such as 3M Super 77.

259 MAKING PROFESSIONAL-LOOKING BUGS

If you wish to make cork bugs that look professional and do not have pits in them, first seal the bugs with Dap filler that is easy to wipe on with your finger. You can do this before or after you glue the bug onto the hook. It is easier after gluing, since the hook makes a little "handle" by which to hold the cork. Make sure that the body is smooth and allow the Dap to cure as per the directions before painting with a primer.

" [Fly fishing] is like any other skill, whether it's the knowledge of the Roy Lopez opening in chess, how to hit a golf ball straight, or put spin on a tennis ball, the sheer pleasure of doing something difficult well."

Conrad Voss Bark
A Fly on the Water (1986)

Chapter 8

Tying Fly Wings: Wet, Dry, Streamer, Saltwater, Bass

260 TYING ON DRY FLY WINGS

When tying on dry fly wings, tie them down with the tips facing forward. Then wrap the thread to the rear, tie on the tail and body material, and wrap the thread forward.

Wrap the body up the hook shank toward the eye of the hook, wrapping over the butt of the wings tied to the hook shank. This also builds up the body diameter slightly at this point to make a more natural tapered look.

Then wrap the thread forward, raise the wings with a bump of thread in front of the wings, and tie in the hackle.

The result makes a very lifelike look. It does not create the problems or lumpy look that would occur if tying on the wings butts forward.

261 MAKING WINGS

To make sure that you have even wings on flies when you make them from waterfowl wing quills, take matched sections from the longer or outside edge of each of matched quills from the two wings. Pick the wing sections from the same part of each quill, and make sure that each wing section is the same width before joining them to the hook shank.

262 PROTECTING DRY FLY HACKLE

To protect dry fly hackle, run a few turns of working thread through the wound hackle. Work the thread in a zigzag path to prevent the thread from catching or binding down any of the hackle fibers while protecting and binding over the base of the wrapped hackle. Two or three turns of thread are about right and provide protection to keep the hackle from damage and becoming undone.

263 DIVIDING UPRIGHT WINGS

Use a bodkin to evenly separate the upright wing in a dry fly when making a divided wing. This allows you to look at the two wings and make sure that they are equal before you criss-cross the thread between them to divide the wing permanently.

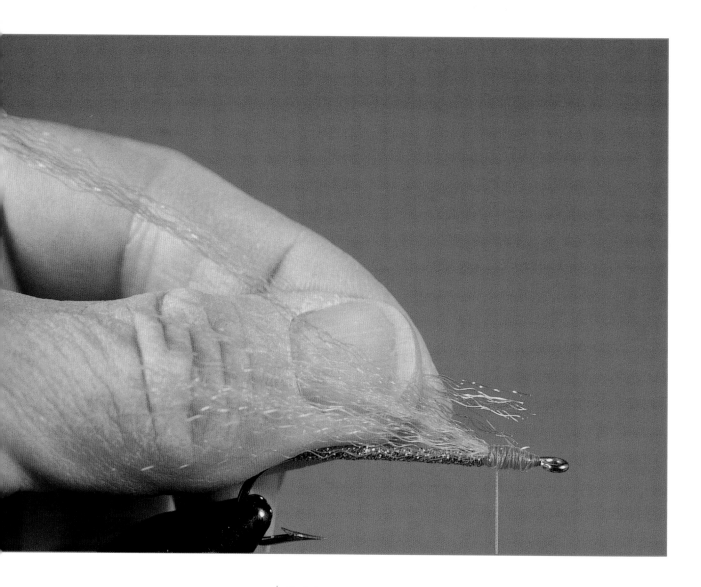

264 TYING DOWN SYNTHETIC STREAMER WINGS: ONE

A problem when tying down synthetic streamer wings is that the synthetic material is often slipperier than natural material (such as bucktail) and thus more likely to slip out after you tie it down. To prevent this, tie down a wing in small bundles, rather than tying the entire wing at once.

The result is that you have separate wraps of thread holding each small bundle of synthetic material. This holds more securely than one overall wrap. It also helps to soak the wrapping thread at this point with head cement or nail polish to penetrate the wrap and secure the wing butts. To make this really secure, add a tiny drop of glue or head cement to each small bundle as you tie it down.

265 TYING DOWN SYNTHETIC STREAMER WINGS: TWO

Another way to secure synthetic streamer wings is to glue the ends of the bundle that you plan to use. There are two ways to do this. One is to coat or dip the end of the bundle before placing it on the hook and tying it down. Then wrap over the wet-glued bundle to secure it in one bunch and to the thread, helping to hold it. A second way is to tie down the bundle and leave the end of the synthetics free. Then add a drop of head cement to the end of this bundle and continue to wrap and finish the tie down of this bundle. Cut off any excess protruding synthetic material. Clean your scissors after doing this.

266 TYING DOWN SYNTHETIC STREAMER WINGS: THREE

A third way to secure synthetics is to prepare your bundle, then touch the tying end of the bundle to a flame to melt it, forming a solid mass or a series of small balls of molten plastic. To do this properly, just barely touch the bundle to the flame, since you want to just barely melt them together, not make a big molten mess. Then place the bundle over the hook shank and tie in place.

A slight lump at the molten end of the bundle helps keep the wing from pulling out from under the thread wrap. This makes a larger head, so do this only on bigger flies.

267 TYING STREAMER WINGS

To get a streamer wing of buck-tail or synthetics tied correctly to the top of the hook shank, hold the butts at an angle to and in front of the hook shank when wrapping the thread over the shank and wing.

Pulling down on the thread slides the wing up into the proper position on top of, and parallel to, the hook shank where you can secure it with subsequent wraps. The result is a properly positioned wing on top of and in line with the hook shank.

268 POSITIONING STREAMER WINGS

To position a streamer wing, make two loose wraps over the wing as you hold it in place on top of the hook shank. Then pull the thread tight and straight down to secure the wing in position on top of the hook shank.

269 VEILING STREAMER WINGS

To make a streamer wing that encircles or "veils" the body, first position the wing on top of the hook shank with two or three light-pressure wraps of thread. Then use your left thumbnail to push down on the top of the wing base to spread the wing fibers around the hook shank and to veil the body. Check that the veiling is even, then wrap tightly.

"Anyone who knows fish knows that pound for pound any salt-water fish is far stronger, far more disinclined to be hauled in on a line than a comparable freshwater fish."

Louis D. Rubin, Jr.
The Even-Tempered Angler (1983)

270 HOLDING STREAMER WINGS

To secure a streamer wing of bucktail or synthetics to the top of a hook shank and keep it in position, make a "reverse" loop wrap. To do this, bring the thread up in front of the hook shank, and then in back, up, over and around the wing. Finish by bringing the thread in back of the hook shank (far side of the hook) and pulling tight.

This wraps like a figure-eight, or infinity sign, to secure the wing on top of the hook shank. Because of the figure-eight loop, the wing is not able to creep down onto the side of the fly and thus destroy the appearance of classic streamer flies.

Finish by making several more wraps of thread around the hook shank and base so that the wing will not twist from its position on top of the hook.

271 DIVIDING WINGS WITH THREAD HARNESS

To divide upright wings when tying dry flies, use a thread harness, as I first learned from the writings of flytier Charles Meck.

For this, first tie down the wings by the butt end with the tips extending forward. Tie them to the upright position. Then take a separate length of tying thread, make a loop around the hook shank in back of the wings, and pull the ends straight up. Pull this thread harness forward and between the divided wings to separate them into two equal bunches of fibers. Pull down just forward of the wings, using enough tension to create the divided look you desire. Tie off this thread harness with the working thread.

You can also make this easier by twisting the thread harness before pulling it forward to divide the wings. This prevents an errant wing fiber from sticking straight up between the thread harness.

272 MOISTENED MARABOU

Marabou is a great, soft attractor material for wings and tails in flies, but also difficult to handle. To make it easier to tie down, moisten the marabou slightly and then bundle the butt ends.

One way to handle the butt ends is to twist the butt end of the moistened marabou to make a tight, skinny bundle for easy tying. Don't wet or soak it if you only want to control the marabou—adding water will rust the hook or make it difficult to handle.

273 USING MARABOU BLOOD FEATHERS

The blood feathers from the stem of marabou (turkey under-feathers) are generally uniformly the same length and thus easy to tie in as a streamer wing. When they are available, most flytiers prefer these to working with the longer marabou feathers where you have to cut the plumy part from the main stem and then carefully fold it into a bundle. To use marabou bloods, trim the butt end and then stroke the feather back as you tie the butt end into the fly.

274 MAKING MARABOU BUNDLES

More marabou is available as stems and feathers than as the smaller and easier-to-use blood plumes. These are harder to handle, since you must cut from the main stem and then craft it into a bundle.

To make these bundles for tying down as a streamer wing, first cut a section from one side of the main stem. Then carefully fold the section over once or twice, creating a bundle—or at least a more easily handled batch of marabou that you can twist or roll into a bundle.

This bundle is then easy to tie onto the hook to make a wing. If necessary, this can be done several times to create a large bundle for tying down one time, or several small bundles that can be tied on one at a time to make a thicker wing.

To keep marabou from tangling around the hook bend or hook shank, mix the marabou with stiffer material such as bucktail, calf tail, or synthetics to give it some structure while still retaining the fluffy movement of the marabou. Do this to create a mixed wing bundle before tying it down on the hook.

Good stiffening materials for this include calf tail or any of the stiffer synthetics such as Super Hair, Ultra Hair, and Fish Hair.

276 ADDING FLASH MATERIAL TO WINGS

Add flash material (Krystal Flash, Crystal Splash, etc.) to the sides of a streamer fly wing by using one bundle that is double the length of the bundle you want on each side. Tie this down on the hook at the middle of the bundle on one side of the fly wing. Then cross the bundle of flash over the top of the hook to the opposite side and wrap with thread again to tie down this side. If necessary, trim the two sides to an equal length.

This method requires less time in preparing the flash on the wing for tying, and creates equal flash bundles for the two sides of the fly.

277 MARKING HACKLES

You can "make" your own specialty hackles using permanent felt-tip markers to color them as you desire.

Today, we use a lot of plain hackle and grizzly hackle, but there are special hackles that have dark center vanes and/or dark outside fibers. You can mark plain hackles the same way, as well as to make grizzly feathers.

To do this, use a permanent felt-tip marker, a ruler, and some scrap paper. Lay each hackle that you want to mark on the paper, and lay the ruler along the part you want to mark. For the center, this would be alongside the main stem, while for the edges it would be along the edge. Then dot or pat the felt-tip maker along the area to be marked. You can't stroke it, since this will only bend the hackle fibers.

For grizzly hackle, hold the ruler at right angles to the feather and mark each section in turn as you move the ruler up the feather. If you like, you can turn the feather over and mark in the same spots for a darker, more pronounced effect. You can do this with any light feather using any color of marker. Black, olive, and brown are the most favored.

278 FLY WINGS FROM ENVELOPES

Tyvek, the material used for insulating houses and to make tough, indestructible envelopes and packaging materials, also makes great fly wings.

One Tyvek envelope provides a lot of material for making wings for dry flies, nymphs, dragonflies, damselflies, terrestrials, hoppers, crickets, etc. You can cut them out with scissors or use one of the punches available from fly shops designed to punch out a pre-formed and shaped wing. Best are wings that are not too large, as large wings of this or similar materials tend to flutter in air currents, affecting casting accuracy.

"The surf: certainly one of nature's finest edges."

Russell Chatham
Dark Waters (1988)

279 EASIER "EVENING" OF BUCKTAIL

To make it easy to stack, or make even, bucktail fibers and similar materials when making streamer wings, add a little talcum powder to the bucktail bundle when adding it to the stacker. The talcum powder makes it easier for the fibers to slide against other fibers when using the stacker.

The best way to do this is to pour a tiny amount of talcum powder into your hand and brush the bucktail or other fur in this puddle of powder. This coats the fibers before adding them to the stacker to make it easy to even the ends.

280 SYNTHETIC STREAMER WINGS

To get a tapered look to a streamer wing of synthetic material (such as Super Hair, Ultra Hair, Unique, and others), use barber thinning scissors to thin the material to make the wing fibers different lengths. This will not taper the individual fibers, but makes the whole wing look tapered and thus more natural and lifelike.

"There is only one secret in dry-fly fishing, which is to make an artificial fly float over a trout in such a way that it looks appetizing enough for him to swallow."

Dermot Wilson
Fishing the Dry Fly (1970)

281 SHEET FOAM WINGS

Thin, packaging sheet foam makes ideal wings on flies, particularly when used as folded wings such as for houseflies, caddis, stoneflies, and extended wings such as are used for dragonfly and damselfly imitations. This material does have a grain to it, just like wood, so tear a small section of it first to determine the grain direction. Then make wings with the long axis of the wing parallel with the grain of the sheet foam. These are easy to cut out with scissors. Note that this material is not as durable as Tyvek or stranded materials used for similar wings.

A Few Miscellaneous Tips

282 SPACING DRY FLIES

Beginners often have trouble making the head on a dry fly. One reason is not leaving enough room to make the head properly without impeding the hook eye or damaging the dry fly hackle.

Older fly books suggested that you leave a small amount of space (about the width of a fly hook eye) between the eye and the front of the wrapped head.

To make a wrapped head properly, tie in the wings at about one-quarter to one-third of the hook shank length in back of the hook eye. This leaves room for the body, along with ample room for the wings and hackle, while providing space for finishing the small tapered head.

283 USING CASSETTE TAPE FOR BACKING

You can tie on simple scud and shrimp carapaces from cassette tape. Cassettes come in both the standard and the mini-tape, with all measuring about 1/8 inch (3 mm) across. Most vary from brown to gray in color. Cut into a convenient length for use, tie down, and segment with spiral wraps of tying thread.

284 CLEARING HEAD CEMENT

It is not uncommon to have head cement clog the eye of a fly, which is why all anglers should carry safety pins or a nipper with a built-in needle to clear the eyes of flies. One way to prevent this is to run a scrap feather or hackle through the eye after tying and sealing to clear out any excess wet sealer. You can use a feather several times for this before the glue makes it ineffective.

285 MAKING TEMPLATES FOR TYING IDENTICAL FLIES

Tying different sizes of the same fly pattern? One way to get consistent results is to make up a simple template or chart that indicates the correct length of tails, wings, hackle, etc. You can do this for dry flies, wet flies, and even for proper wing and tail length on streamers and bucktails. You can get these measurements from some books on fly tying, tools that attach to the fly-tying vise that are made for measuring hackle and tails, or from the chart listed on page 115.

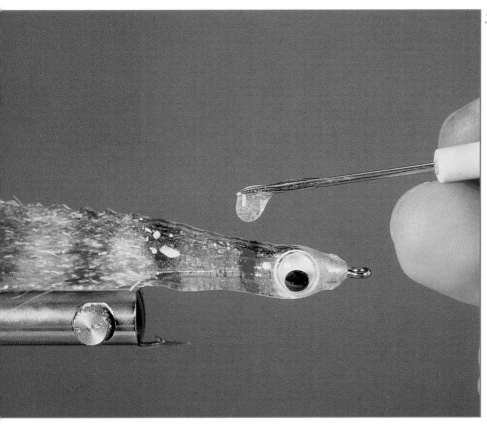

286 USING EPOXY FINISH

Epoxy finish is best for large flies, flies with larger heads, or where you want a very durable fly when fishing for tough or toothy fish. To make an epoxy head, best results are from clear, five-minute epoxy glue, mixed thoroughly and applied evenly to the fly head. Most epoxies turn slightly yellow in time, so don't make up too many flies in advance.

287 ANT IMITATIONS

When tying ants, make sure to maintain a thin, distinct "waist" on the fly and keep separate the thorax and abdomen parts. In some flies, such as the McMurray's Ant, this is pretty obvious, but use care when tying ants built up on the hook shank with thread, yarn, or floss. The separation of both parts and a wide waist helps the trout to recognize this as an ant and not a beetle—not that beetles won't catch fish!

288 MIXING EPOXY

Mix epoxy on a white card or paper, stirring the two parts evenly to eliminate the visible swirls in the glue, and apply to the head of the fly with a bodkin.

289 ELIMINATING BUBBLES IN EPOXY

Mixing epoxy glue for coating fly heads or other fly-tying purposes can cause bubbles. To eliminate the bubbles, spread and mix the epoxy and breathe on the epoxy puddle. Your breath will break any bubbles that have formed.

290 PREVENTING EPOXY SAGGING

To prevent epoxy heads on flies from sagging, place the fly on a fly rotator that slowly (five to twenty turns per minute) rotates flies as the epoxy cures. These fly rotators are available in AC or battery styles from any fly shop or catalog house. You can also make your own.

To make your own, rig a low-rpm motor on a stand and add a large foam ring or disk into which you can hook flies. Good motors for the purpose are those for hobbies or used for turning a barbecue spit.

291 DRY FLY

Height of wings = shank length of hook

Height (radius) of hackle = 3/4 of the shank length of hook

Tail = length of entire hook, less eye (shank length + bend)

Body length (from tail to hackle) = 3/4 of shank length of hook

292 WET FLY

Body = shank length of hook, less wrapped head

Wings = shank length of hook + bend of hook, less wrapped fly head

Tail = body length (shank length of hook, less wrapped fly head)

Hackle = distance from wrapped fly head to point of hook

293 STREAMER FLY

Wing = 1 1/4 to 2 times the shank length of hook

Tail = 1/3 of the shank length of the hook, less the wrapped fly head, or to meet the end of the wing

Body = shank length of the hook, less the wrapped fly head

Shoulders = 1/3 of the shank length of the hook, less the wrapped fly head

Cheek = 1/4 the shank length of the hook, less the wrapped fly head

Throat = 1/2 the shank length of the hook, less the wrapped fly head

(The above streamer fly approximations are from the author, since no established standard exists.)

"*Fishing always reaches its peak at a time when the bugs are thickest. And bugs are thickest at the places where fishing is best....So whenever and wherever you enjoy good fishing you can expect to find mosquitoes, black flies, midges, or deerflies, all lusting for your life's blood.*"

H. G. Tapply
The Sportsman's Notebook (1964)

294 VARYING YOUR PALMERING

When palmering a fly body with a spiral wrap of hackle, you can vary the look of the fly. To make a very bushy fly, use close spirals to build up hackle bulk. To make a spare, straggly body, use wide turns of the hackle.

Realize that if you make a very bushy palmering wrap, you might have to use more than one hackle feather. You can do this by tying two or more hackle feathers to the hook shank, then wrap up the hook shank.

A second way to do this is to tie on one hackle and wrap it to the end of the hackle, then tie in a second hackle as you tie off the first. Continue this way to create a bushy palmering until you reach the head of the fly.

Regardless of how you do it, the several hackles make a bushy palmering, even if not wrapped in a tight spiral.

If you want a very sparse palmering for a different look, space the spirals of the hackle far apart.

295 CATERPILLARS

If palmering hackle to make surface- or subsurface-caterpillar fly imitations, consider using larger-than-normal hackle and then trimming it all around. The result is a blunter, more visible hackle that closely resembles the short, fuzzy projections found on most caterpillars. You can also trim it in different ways, such as leaving it long on the sides and short on the top and bottom, or long at one or both ends and short in the middle. These more closely approximate the appearance of a live caterpillar.

296 PROTECTING PALMERED HACKLES

To protect palmered hackle and make a fly more durable, wind a spiral wrap of tying thread through the hackle. Leave a long tag end of tying thread when starting the fly, add other materials/hackle, and wrap the thread and hackle forward. Follow this by a spiral wrap of thread over and through the palmered hackle. For best results, make this wrap in the opposite direction (from back to front, rather than from front to back around the hook), over the previously palmered hackle.

297 MAKING TUBING EELS

Eels are a staple food for a lot of inshore saltwater and larger fresh-water gamefish. To make a simple eel, Brian Owens of CT came up with the idea of using velvet tubing available from sewing and fabric stores. The thin-wall cloth tubing, about 1/2 inch (13 mm) thick, is available in black, white, red, and maroon. You can color the back of white eels with permanent felt-tip markers to make them more eel-like. Good colors are black for the back and olive for the upper sides.

To "tie" these, cut several inches of tubing and remove the internal cord. Run the hook through the open end and then out the side. Place the hook in a vise, tie on the thread, and tie down the open end to finish the eel. Complete by sealing the tail end with fabric glue. You can make similar smaller eels using bolo cord also available from sewing stores or white parachute cord, available from outdoor stores.

298 FLATTENED FLY SKELETONS

Nymphs are often flat to best resist water pressure and currents. This is true for both small nymphs and the larger nymphs such as hellgrammites and western stoneflies.

For larger flies, make them by tying down a flat "skeleton" board to the hook, and then gluing the flat skeleton to the hook for stability. With this skeleton tied and glued in place, wrap over the skeleton with body material to make the desired nymph pattern.

Good skeleton material for wrapping onto a hook includes the plastic used in flexible hook boxes (such as Mustad), strips of strapping material used to pack and ship boxes, and any suitable flat, clear plastic from blister-packed products.

An easy way to tie this on is to cut a notch on both sides of each end. This leaves a small nib in the center of each end to tie onto the hook before the thread is spiral wrapped around the rest of the skeleton and before you epoxy it in place.

299 TYING SIMPLE CHUM FLIES

You can tie simple chum flies to catch saltwater fish when chumming, by using a single wrap of crosscut rabbit strip, then tying off with a neat head and sealing with epoxy. Make the fly more durable for toothy fish, such as bluefish, by tying down the tag end of the rabbit strip, then coating the hook shank with epoxy glue, wrapping the thread up the hook shank, and then following with the crosscut rabbit strip. Then make the head, finish and seal the head with epoxy.

This method seals the wrapped rabbit strip into a bed of epoxy so that no toothy fish can cut it off or damage it. Toothy species can still fray the fur, but they can't cut the fly apart.

300 MAKING GERBUBBLE BUGS

To make Gerbubble bugs, which have a side hackle extending from the blocky body, use a Dremel tool and a small cutting wheel to cut the slot around the border of the cork, balsa, or foam body into which you can glue hackle, marabou, or Body Fur.

Hackle was originally used in this 1930s bass bug, but marabou provides more action while Body Fur is an easy-to-use synthetic.

301 HANDLING BULLET HEADS ON FLIES

The Thunder Creek series of flies have a bullet head in which the wing (usually bucktail) is tied forward and then reversed over the body. It is then tied off about one-third the shank length in back of the hook eye to make a gill pattern.

To make these easy to tie and to form the bullet head, use a large plastic straw to reverse and push the bucktail from the forward position to the rear. To tie it off, push the straw into the bucktail bundle from the side, arrange it so that the bucktail surrounds the straw, and then push the straw back over the hook.

The reason for pushing the straw into the bundle from the side is to prevent bucktail from ending up in the lumen of the straw as might happen if you pushed it on from the front end. You can leave the straw in place while you tie down the bucktail (do not tie down the straw) or hold the bucktail bundle with the fingers of your left hand as you wrap the bucktail.

If you want a more permanent bullet-head pusher, buy a length of metal tubing from a hobby shop. You can get these in aluminum, copper, brass, and PVC plastic. They are available in different diameters, from about 1/8 inch (3.2 mm) and larger, so that you can have different-diameter pushers for different-size flies.

302 PLASTIC TUBING MINNOWS

A neat way to make minnow-like flies for warm water and saltwater use is to use synthetic plastic tubing material such as E-Z Body or Corsair. Both of these are braided, open tubing materials that come in a variety of sizes and colors for making all types of streamer flies.

Slide them over the body of the fly with the wing or tail materials extending from the rear. To make these materials flat to simulate the flat side of minnows such as silver-sides, dace, anchovies, etc., iron the material before using it. Do this on a hard surface such as a kitchen counter, not a soft ironing board. When doing this, make sure that you set the iron to a medium setting and that the iron does not harm the countertop. Hold the tubing at both ends (you might need help in holding one end) and then iron a length of the tubing, which you can later cut into short lengths for individual flies.

" If, as I suspect, trout fishing is something of a disease, then it is also something of a therapy in itself."

Tom Sutcliffe, M.D.
Reflections on Fishing
(1990)

303 TYING PLASTIC TUBE MINNOWS

Many minnow patterns are possible by using a body of plastic tubing (E-Z Body, Corsair, Gudebrod G-Tubing). A simple way to tie these is to cut a length of the tubing, slide it onto a long-shaft bobbin, and then tie on the thread and a wing/tail of bucktail or synthetics. Then slide the body tubing up onto the hook shank, covering the forward part of the wing/tail, and tie down with the bobbin. This prevents tying off and tying back on again.

304 RATTLING BEADS ON A FLY

Rattles help fish to find flies, particularly in stained or murky water. Rattles of plastic, glass, or aluminum are available for tying into flies, but you can also use sliding beads, in a suggestion from flytier George Liros.

For this, first slide two loose metal beads onto a long shank hook (bend the barb down first). Then begin to tie, but start the fly about halfway down the hook shank. Tie the fly you want (usually a streamer fly) and finish the fly, gluing the rear bead to the hook shank and the wrapped head. Allow the forward bead to slide free.

When fishing, use twitches so that the fly falls head first, while a twitch pulls it up to cause the forward bead to slide back and strike the rear bead to make noise.

305 ALIGNING BUCKTAIL BY HAND

If you don't have a stacker to align the ends of bucktail when making deer-hair bugs or tying saltwater or streamer wings, you can do it by hand. To do this, first pull out and remove the long, errant fibers that stick out from the bundle of fur. Then spread the bundle out flat, grab the longest fibers, and gently pull them out. Do this so as to not disturb the other fibers in the bundle. Then replace these fibers in the bundle, making sure that the ends match those already in the bundle. Check the bundle and do this several times until all of the fibers are about the same length and suitable for tying into the fly.

"Any meticulous attention to color or detail [in a fly pattern] is wasted effort."

Vincent C. Marinaro
In the Ring of the Rise (1976)

306 GLUING CRABS

Crabs can be made by gluing together two parts (carapace and abdomen) with the hook and legs between the two parts. Often the best carapace and abdomen includes foam, fuzzy foam, vinyl, and similar flat waterproof materials.

To make sure that these materials glue well, use small doll-size clothespins to hold the two body parts tightly together while the glue cures. Doll-size clothespins are available from toy stores.

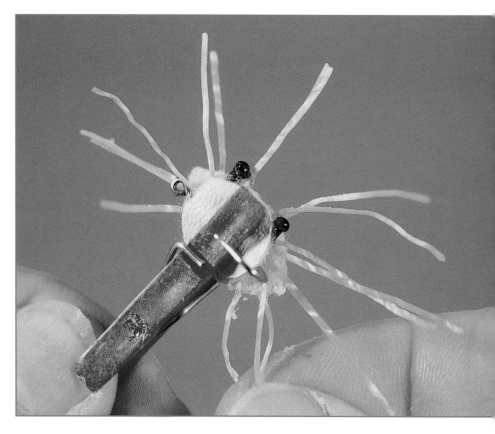

307 REINFORCING FLY SHOULDERS

Anglers use feathers such as those from guinea fowl to make shoulders on some flies. These shoulders are further dressed with a painted-on eye. This is a traditional method of tying some streamers in a Northeast style.

To make this easy to do, first coat the shoulder feathers with a clear sealer such as Softex, Flexament, or Loon Soft Head Cement. This also reinforces the shoulder to make it more durable. Then paint the eyes on the shoulder using different-size nail or pin heads to dot the eye and the pupil on the feather. The clear coating protects the feather from damage and prevents the paint of the eye from running or bleeding into the feather.

308 ADDING GLITTER TO FLY HEADS

For a little more flash on your large warm water or saltwater flies, add standard or micro glitter to the epoxy when making the epoxy head.

To do this, first add the glitter to either the "A" or "B" (catalyst/hardener or resin) portion of the epoxy, mix thoroughly, and then mix with the other part. This step is particularly important if using a five-minute epoxies. Note that you will dilute the glitter you add to just one part when you mix it with the second equal part of the glue. Mix thoroughly and add to the fly, then place the fly on a rotator.

Craft shops carry glitter.

309 CRANE FLY IMITATIONS

Tie in a short body and then a very large hackle to simulate the long legs of these ungainly insects to create a simple crane fly imitation.

These large crane flies are a lesser, but still important, food source for trout, and a few of these can work wonders when fishing in the evening hours during the summer months. In essence, these are like the variant patterns of flies that are tied with extended tails and oversize hackles.

310 MAKING POM-POM GLO BUGS

You can make great glo bugs for trout, salmon, and steelhead fishing without tying and cutting material as is called for in most fly-tying books. For this, visit a craft store and buy some pom-poms in the right size and color. If you cannot get pom-poms in the color desired, you can buy white pom-poms and dye them pink or orange with Rit or Tintex.

To use these pom-poms, impale the center of the pompom with the hook point and then force the pom-pom around the hook bend and shank. To avoid sticking yourself, use care when doing this.

Place the pom-pom on a scrap of wood and then push the hook point down on the center of the pom-pom. Once the hook point and barb are through the pom-pom, then you can slide the pom-pom around on the hook shank.

To keep the pom-pom in place on the hook, first wrap the hook shank center with tying thread, tie off, and soak the thread with epoxy or CA glue before finally sliding the pom-pom into place on the center of the hook.

311 MAKING BULLET-HEAD FLIES

To make the most effective bullet-head (Thunder Creek style) patterns, use some light-colored bucktail or fur for the belly of the fly and dark-colored bucktail or fur for the back of the fly.

To keep these separate for later folding over the hook shank to form the wing, use a separate length of tying thread to loosely wrap around the forward part of the bundle to keep it separate from the subsequent bundle. Thus, if first tying down the light-colored belly, wrap some thread or cord around it, and then tie down the darker-colored back fibers or bucktail.

Next, wrap the thread back to the tie-down position and fold the back fibers over the hook shank and tie them in place. This is easy since the belly fibers are separate and loosely wrapped in a thread bundle.

Then remove the thread wrap over the belly fibers, fold that back, and tie in place with the working thread at the same spot.

312 NETTING FOR FLOAT PODS, TRAILING SHUCKS

To hold a tiny float pod of foam onto a fly as a parachute post or trailing shuck, use a piece of old stocking to hold the pod into place. Use sheer stocking material, or a color that matches the color needed for your fly. Cut the stocking material into small squares. Place the foam float pod into the center of a square and then wrap the stocking material tightly around it. Then tie the "neck" of this bundle onto the hook shank, secure it with thread, and then continue with the rest of the fly. The result is a tightly secured float pod, parachute post, or trailing shuck that will not come apart.

313 GLUING JUNGLE COCK TO SHOULDERS

To add jungle cock eyes to a shoulder feather, such as silver pheasant, glue them in place to make tying easier. First assemble a number of the shoulder feathers, place them separately on your workbench, and then glue a jungle cock feather to form an eye on the shoulder. Use flexible cement for this, such as Flexament or similar flexible fly-tying glue. Do this with a bunch of feathers and jungle cocks so that you have them ready when tying a particular fly. This is particularly good when tying freshwater dace patterns.

314 MAKING SHRIMP ANTENNAE

To make antennae for shrimp flies, you can use thin monofilament, dyed black. To do this, dye a spool of 12- to 20-pound (5.4- to 9.1-kg) mono with black Rit or Tintex dye, or buy a spool of black or dark-dyed mono. To create the antennae effect on a shrimp fly, tie in a few strands of the mono and leave them long, as they are on a real shrimp. You can use more than two (the number on a live shrimp) since fish cannot count. You only want to create the impression of the antennae, so a half-dozen strands are not too many. Another possibility is to use a few strands of black Super Hair, twisted and held together with soft glue such as Ultra Flex, Flexament, or Softex.

"Now and then fishermen get excited about a fly that has been 'outlawed' in England or the Sahara Desert. That fly is said to be a wicked killer."

Arthur R. Macdougall, Jr.
"The Best Fly Is Not Yet"
The Trout Fisherman's Bedside Book (1963)

Author Acknowledgments

Anyone who has read the acknowledgments of my previous books might find this section a little repetitious. There is a reason for that, since many of my friends over several decades have helped me in all aspects of fishing and its related hobbies and activities. These include all types of fishing from fly to surf to offshore to bass; all types of fly tying for fresh and saltwater species; rigging boats for fishing; and making rods, lures, and other tackle; etc.

These include friends such as Chuck Edghill, Lefty Kreh, Mark Sosin, Norm Bartlett, Ed Russell, Art Scheck, Dave Klausmeyer, Bill May, Jim Heim, Joe Zimmer, Jack Goellner, and so many others. I have been honored by their friendship and grateful for their patience and help over the years with my writing for various magazines and books. They have all put up with me, taught me much about fly fishing and fly tying, and been unstinting with their help and shared experience. To them all, I owe a debt of thanks that is impossible to repay.

As with past books, I owe special thanks to Chuck Edghill. Chuck read this manuscript to check for grammatical, factual, and typing errors; his efforts resulting in a far better book than it would have been otherwise. Chuck is an experienced and dedicated angler (fly fishing and all types of other fishing), a precise and knowledgeable flytier (and once commercial tyer), and an excellent editor who gave his time and talent to make this book better. This is also not new for Chuck, since he has given before of his time in editing and improving my other books, including the companion to this, Complete Photo Guide to Fly Fishing. Thank you, Chuck, for your generosity. Naturally, any mistakes that remain are my fault and responsibility alone.

In addition, I have (as we all do) picked up ideas from a number of publications over the years, including Fly Fisherman, Fly Tyer, American Angler in particular, but also a host of other magazines in the fly fishing/fly tying genre or general fishing magazines with fly fishing/tying coverage or columns. Books, too, have always been an interest of mine, and there is a plethora of books on all aspects of fly fishing, fly tying, and tying for particular geographic regions and specific species. Seminars, too, have lead to an influx of ideas and techniques from which I have gained much.

Also, I give credit to an old man who 50-odd years ago took a boy under his wing to teach him about the fishing of which the boy's parents and family knew nothing. Fred Klemcke was about 60 and I was about 11 when my parents moved to a home adjoining his property. He was a retired cavalry officer and combat veteran of four years of trench warfare in World War I, fighting for Kaiser Wilhelm and Germany. He moved to the United States, worked in the import/export business, fished, and tied flies.

I later learned that during the war (before I knew him), neighbors noted his light on late at night through the winter months and thought he was a spy sending secret messages to Berlin and the Third Reich. Nope, he was just tying flies for the coming trout season. His friendship and help over the several years before he retired and moved to Maine taught me about fishing, fly fishing and fly casting, trout fishing, and yes, fly tying.

It was during one Christmas that he gave me my first vise (a Herter's) along with the related tools and enough materials and hooks to get me started. He had previously taught me the rudiments of tying. From that and fishing with him my love grew for not only fishing, but for the skill and art of fly tying. Unfortunately, he died before I started writing, and before he knew that he had laid the foundation and given me the groundwork for the life I enjoy today, and have enjoyed for decades.

I give my thanks also to my editor Barbara Harold and her staff at Creative Publishing international for seeing the value of this book as a companion to my book, Complete Photo Guide to Fly Fishing.

Finally, my thanks to my wife, Brenda, who puts up with me when I prevail upon her for a fishing photo that I need, my visits to craft stores for fly-tying materials, time talking with friends about the esoteric aspects of the fly-fishing sport and the fly-tying hobby, and time at the computer writing about these things that consume my life. To her, my thanks for her patience, forbearance, and understanding, in this as with all things in our shared lives.

Boyd Pfeiffer

Further Reading

Best, A. K. *Production Fly Tying,* Boulder, CO, Pruett Publishing Co., 1989, 175 Pages

Borger, Gary. *Designing Trout Flies,* Wausau, WI, Tomorrow River Press, 1991, 214 Pages

Bruce, Joe. *Fly Design Theory & Practice,* Lisbon, MD, K & D Publishing, 2002, 111 Pages

Fullum, Jay "Fishy." *Fishy's Flies,* Mechanicsburg, PA, Stackpole Books, 2002, 68 Pages

Hughes, Dave. *Trout Flies, The Tier's Reference,* Mechanicsburg, PA, Stackpole Books, 1999, 470 Pages

Klausmeyer, David. *Guide Flies,* Woodstock, VT, The Countryman Press, 2003, 118 Pages

—. *Tying Contemporary Saltwater Flies,* Woodstock, VT The Countryman Press, 2002, 152 Pages

Kreh, Lefty. *Saltwater Fly Patterns,* New York, NY, Lyons & Burford, 1995, 211 Pages

Lafontaine, Gary. *Trout Flies, Proven Patterns,* Helena, MT, Greycliff Publishing, 1993, 260 Pages

Leeson, Ted and Schollmeyer, Jim. *The Fly Tier's Benchside Reference,* Portland, OR, Frank Amato Publications, 1998, 444 Pages

Likakis, John M. *Bass Bug Basics,* Woodstock, VT, Countryman Press, 2003, 86 Pages

Martin, Darrel. *Fly-Tying Methods,* New York, NY, Nick Lyons Books, 1987, 276 Pages

Meck, Charles. *101 Innovative Fly-Tying Tips,* Guilford, CT, The Lyons Press, 2002, 192 Pages

Moore, Wayne. *Fly Tying Notes,* Seattle, WA, Recreational Consultants, 1984, 93 Pages

Morris, Skip. *Tying Foam Flies,* Portland, OR, Frank Amato Publications, 1994, 47 Pages

Morris, Skip. *The Art of Tying the Bass Fly,* Portland, OR, Frank Amato Publications, 1996, 88 Pages

Pfeiffer, C. Boyd. *Bug Making,* New York, NY, Lyons and Burford, 1993, 271 Pages

—. *Fly Fishing Bass Basics,* Mechanicsburg, PA, Stackpole Books, 1997, 168 Pages

—. *Fly Fishing Saltwater Basics,* Mechanicsburg, PA, Stackpole Books, 1999, 232 Pages

—. *Shad Fishing,* Mechanicsburg, PA, Stackpole Books, 2002, 226 Pages

—. *Simple Flies,* Woodstock, VT, The Countryman Press, 2005,

—. *Tying Trout Flies,* Iola, WI, Krause Publications, 2002, 160 Pages

—. *Tying Warmwater Flies,* Iola, WI, Krause Publications, 2003, 160 Pages

Scheck, Art. *Tying Better Flies,* Woodstock, VT, The Countryman Press, 2003, 173 Pages

Schollmeyer, Jim. *Nymph Fly-Tying Techniques,* Portland, OR, Frank Amato Publications, 2001, 125 Pages

Schollmeyer, Jim and Leeson, Ted. *Tying Emergers,* Portland, OR, Frank Amato Publications, 2004, 344 Pages

—. *Inshore Flies,* Portland, OR, Frank Amato Publications, 2000, 87 Pages

Steeves, Harrison R., Jr. *Tying Flies with Foam, Fur and Feathers,* Mechanicsburg, PA, Stackpole Books, 2003, 136 Pages

Stewart, Dick. *Fly-Tying Tips,* Intervale, NH, Northland Press Inc. 1990, 93 Pages

Talleur, Dick. *The Versatile Fly Tyer,* New York, NY, Nick Lyons Books, 1990, 339 Pages

Tryon, Chuck and Sharon. *Figuring Out Flies,* Rolla, MO, Ozark Mountain Fly Anglers, 1990, 182 Pages

Veniard, John and Downs, Donald. *Fly-Tying Problems and Their Answers,* New York, NY, Crown Publishers, 1972, 124 Pages

Veverka, Bob. *Innovative Saltwater Flies,* Mechanicsburg, PA, Stackpole Books, 1999, 197 Pages

Williamson, Robert. *Creative Flies Innovative Tying Techniques,* Portland, OR. Frank Amato Publications, 2002, 40 Pages

INDEX

Creative Publishing international
is your complete source of How-to information for the Outdoors.

Available Outdoor Titles:

The Complete
FLY FISHERMAN™